# The Virginia Valley

A Novel by
Douglas Malcolm

Cover portrait illustration by Darrin Fuller.

ISBN: 0615992536
ISBN 13: 9780615992532
Library of Congress Control Number: 2014905522
LightSeeker Media, Gibsonia, PA

Dedicated to slaves who lie in unmarked graves.

# Chapter 1

In 1817 in the town of Kilkenny, Ireland, Aidan Smith was born into a family of "smiths." He could never say whether he took to blacksmithing because he had the powerful physique to do it, or if it was the work that made him so strong. But he knew from the first time he saw his father raise popping, orange sparks with a bellows that it was the only work he'd ever want to do.

Aidan was forced to leave his native land just before the scourge of the potato famine blackened it. Many speculate as to what caused Ireland's dreaded potato blight. Some say it was carried on the feet of those just off a foreign ship. Some wonder if it was borne on a fateful breeze. And more than a few think it spewed forth from the very gates of hell for all the tragedy that it carried. Regardless of the source, the blight took half the potato crop in 1845, and most of what was planted in the two years that followed.

The blight, and the way that Aidan's countrymen were treated by the English, were enough to literally starve the country to death. If they had been free to own more land, they would have had a fighting chance. But Irish commoners were forbidden by the crown to own more than five acres per household. So they set upon the ill-fated potato as their mainstay crop, because the spud produced the highest yield possible from their tiny plots of land.

If there was a fate worse than starvation, it was visited upon those poor souls who fled the blight on "coffin ships" bound for America. Profiteers assembled these deceitful craft in such haste and shoddiness as to make them unable to face a gale without breaking apart in the open sea. Untold families, still hoping to escape sure death on land, died in each other's arms as the cold, gray Atlantic drug them down.

Although Aidan avoided that fate, he did endure a particularly crushing loss.

When he first came of age, he had already been enjoying success in his trade. Then he succeeded in wooing a wonderful mate. He had loved her ever since he first beheld her girlish face ringed in auburn hair. She was, and always would be, his beloved Louisa. Louisa was only sixteen and Aidan five years older when they wed. They lived happily together on love, and what they revered as the Lord's blessings.

It was not long before the second great joy in their lives arrived, a strapping young lad they called "Jack."

Five years passed without another child appearing. Then one night Louisa sauntered into their bedchamber and asked, "Aidan Smith, would ye change anythin' in our lives if ye could?"

He cocked his head and pondered, as he studied the anticipation on her face.

Then it struck him. "Aye! I'd arrange for Jackie ta have a playmate."

Louisa hopped into bed beside him, and replied, "Well, God willin', I believe I have it in me power ta grant ye that wish."

Several happy months later, Louisa and Aidan ventured to a special concert of singing at their cathedral, St. Canice's. They enjoyed the evening very much. Afterward, because carrying the child had become hard on Louisa, Aidan decided to splurge and hire a little hack to carry them back to their rented home.

Time and again, Aidan would try to recall how much time had passed between the moment he left Louisa standing by the cathedral's old tower, and when three "gentlemen" stumbled upon her. The answer always came out the same. It was only an instant. But that was long enough for those three, full to their cups, to try to take liberties with his dear wife. They jostled her roughly until Louisa screamed, "Aidan!" As he charged around a corner, he saw their hands crudely groping her.

"Swine!" he shouted as he dove at the first of them and threw him aside.

Then one of the other two raised his cane and sneered, "I'll put thee in thy place, knave!"

But Aidan beat him to it and delivered a terrible blow to the side of his head. It cartwheeled the drunkard nearly ten feet through the air! Then he flopped, like a rag doll, and didn't move. The world seemed to stop for an instant as they all stared at man's silent form.

Aidan knew in his heart, "*He's dead.*"

When that fact was confirmed, another just as serious emerged as one of the man's companions pronounced, "You'll swing from the gallows, now, peasant. You've gone and murdered a baron." That sealed Aidan and Louisa's fate.

Their vicar, who had always been a dear friend and ally of Aidan's family, stood up in the courts on his behalf in a true and tireless fashion. And the solicitor Louisa hired as Aidan languished in prison worked with all available means to lighten the sentence.

Louisa visited Aidan every time she was permitted. She put off telling him until she had no other choice, "Darlin', ye should know. The costs for the solicitor and the fees of the court have taken all that we'd saved for our cottage."

In the end, the best result their men could gain was to have Louisa, Aidan, their unborn child and Jack make the hazardous voyage to America and be sold there, to labor as indentured servants. The judicial reasoning seemed to be that if Aidan were kept out of sight of the aristocracy, he could pay penance for a number of years, then walk free in a new land. He was forbidden to ever set foot in Ireland again.

Indentured servitude had all but disappeared by then. Many years earlier, there had been thousands of Irish that manned the tobacco fields of Virginia before African slaves replaced them. Still, there was a ship's captain sailing from Dublin who was willing to take Aidan and his family across on speculation. He knew that, because Aidan had a useful trade, he could sell them into servitude and recoup a tidy profit.

When he had some time to consider the prospect, Aidan told Louisa this arrangement was, "Really our only choice, me love."

To that she replied, "We'll just have ta pray, then, that it proves ta be a blessin'."

# Chapter 2

Aidan would never forget the expression on Louisa's face when they first boarded *The Vigilance* in Dublin, and were led roughly below to their "quarters." Any expectations they had about comfort and privacy in the steerage class were rudely obliterated at once.

All of the other passengers on the lower deck were assigned family "bunks" stacked three high against either side of the hull. But because the Smiths were a last minute addition to the full passenger list, they were relegated to a straw-strewn floor in a dim corner, close to a livestock pen.

In their first hours onboard, Aidan and Louisa attempted to hang garments and bed clothes on a rope to create a private room. The air was soon so close and foul, though, that they pulled everything down in order not to suffocate.

Then, as *The Vigilance* began to enter the open sea, all but the most seasoned hands vomited the very bile from their stomachs. The creaking pitch and yaw of the filthy craft drew a nauseating chorus of sobs and groaning that never ceased.

Decorum of any kind disintegrated within the first twenty-four hours. People too weak to reach a slop bucket were reduced to wallowing in their own filth. Babes wailed and parents shouted, as the ghastly voyage rocked fearfully out onto an unruly sea.

Aidan and his family had come aboard with whatever provisions they could carry. They had hoped, in vain, that the ship's steward would at least let them purchase some sustenance, once underway. But by late in the second week their supplies were dwindling. And, as always was her way, Louisa took pity on the poorest and weakest among them. She shared what little she had with those most in need.

Aidan constantly pleaded, "Consider the baby, me love."

Louisa would pretend to nod in agreement. But countless times, as Aidan awoke from another nauseous dream, he'd find Louisa just returning from a mission of mercy. Then he would look out on a tangled maze of wretched beings and see some grateful, weary face showing thanks. He came to realize that Louisa greatly denied herself in order to do this. But by the third week, it truly didn't matter. They were all starving.

Their sole relief from the sickening stench came on Monday mornings when they were quickly herded topside. Crewmen stayed below and swept away the filthy straw. Then they hurled buckets of seawater and lye across the grimy deck and gave it a half-hearted slosh with their mops.

Such brief attempts at sanitation couldn't prevent a pair of deadly diseases from attacking starving bodies. Typhus, carried by lice, and dysentery swept throughout the lower deck. The frail passengers lasted no more than a few days from the onset of these diseases. Aidan watched in fear as poor Jack began to wither from his normal strong health. But it was Louisa who concerned him the most. He'd never seen her skin so pale, almost gray, in the gloom of that floating hellhole.

Finally, the captain ordered they be fed a cup of gruel each morning. It was so foul and worm-infested, that few could eat it and none could keep it down.

When those on the steerage deck thought things couldn't get worse, a new evil emerged. It was announced by the heavy footfall of the onerous first mate. He and his rat-like minions patrolled three times daily for signs of anyone approaching death's door. Somewhat cautiously at first, but then with brazen disdain for the feelings of loved ones, the crewmen drug both the dead and dying topside.

The first mate kept the victim's kin at bay at sword's point as he shouted, "That one's beyond help. Let 'em go!"

Families were not permitted to go on deck to witness the sea "burials." Surely, that prohibition was because the bodies were tossed overboard with no more dignity than flinging a sack of garbage into the sea. Aidan tried to comfort the mourners by reading to them from his Bible.

After two days of not having a crumb of food in their bellies, Louisa said she could try to nurse Jack with the baby's milk. That blessing sustained Jack for about three days more. But as her strength dwindled, so did Louisa's supply. After that, all she could do was wrap her frail arms around her son and try to comfort him.

One night, five days before the ship's lookout finally sighted land, the normal, harsh pitch of the ship settled into a soothing, easy roll. The effect upon the Smiths and their fellow passengers was like that of a babe resting in a gently rocking cradle.

In their first display of mercy or any concern for the poorest passengers, two crewmen left a card game long enough to open the forward hatches. A pleasant, salty breeze drifted down through the lower deck.

"Oh my," sighed Louisa. "I don't think I've ever smelled anythin' as lovely."

Aidan had been lying between Louisa and Jack, holding their hands, and praying that they all would survive. The pleasantness of the breeze inspired him to rummage through a sack and produce the last inch of candle they had, and three damp matches.

It took time, but when he finally succeeded in lighting the candle, Aidan cupped his hand around the flame because the warm breeze made it dance and flicker. Louisa turned and looked at him with approval, as Aidan saw the light glistening in her eyes. He lay back down as he cradled the candle on the matchbox.

What happened next was the sole sweetness of their journey. Without forethought, and despite the fact that it was the dead of summer, Louisa, then Jack and Aidan began to sing "Silent Night." Aidan handed Louisa the candle, reached into the satchel, and drew out his fiddle and bow. He softly played the song's melody. Soon they were joined by a voice from out in the shadows, and then another.

Gradually, singing spread throughout the entire hold. Brittle voices, sobbing, haunting in their weariness somehow blended into a heartfelt chorus for the Savior's ears.

As the nub of candle began to burn Louisa's hand, she grudgingly blew it out. The singing continued another moment. Aidan struck one last note on the fiddle. Then their little family instinctively cuddled together before drifting off to sleep.

Jack said, "I liked the singing, Momma and Papa."

"Mm," replied Louisa, as she weakly squeezed Aidan's hand goodnight.

Several restful hours passed. Then Aidan was struck by sudden fear when he realized Louisa's hand had grown cold! He looked over at Jack and found him asleep. Then he gently released Jack's hand and moved to place his ear upon Louisa's breast.

He heard nothing. So Aidan moved his hand first and then his mouth and nose to just beneath her nostrils. There was no sensation of breath.

As quietly as he could, he tried to jostle her, but nothing. He tried again, and again with more force, and again! Aidan began to sob and shake as his withered insides contorted with an agonizing cramp that made him fight to stifle a painful scream.

As he tried to keep from believing the unthinkable, he draped his arms around Louisa and embraced her lifeless body. She had become so emaciated. He parted her dress around her shrunken stomach and strained to hear any sound of life from within. His attempt was met with cold silence.

Finally, Aidan lay back down beside Louisa and retook her hand and Jack's. As the overwhelming agony of her loss gripped him, he was unable to do anything but shiver and softly weep.

Somewhere in the wee hours, Aidan drifted off again, only to be jolted awake by the crushing heel of the first mate's boot! He could feel Louisa's hand being ripped from his as a sharp sword point pressed at his throat.

"Don't move, preacher man! She's gone, and that's the end of it!" the first mate growled.

Much later, Aidan thanked God for his weakened state at that moment. Otherwise, the weight of that grimy boot would never have kept him from running himself through on cold steel that would have left Jack an orphan.

"Papa! What are they doing? Where are they taking Momma? Why can't she talk?" Jack cried.

From that moment, all that mattered to Aidan Smith was his son, his faith, and how they would survive.

# Chapter 3

Aidan tried to comfort Jack.

"She's in a better place, now. Momma isn't sick anymore. She's not hungry, and she's happy bein' with Jesus."

"Is she happier than she was bein' with us? And why does Jesus need her more than we do? Doesn't he want us to be happy, too?" a bewildered Jack pleaded.

So they passed hours, talking about God's mysteries and how, in the end, they would know all the answers why. Of course, those words were impossible for a child to fully understand. But saying them aloud, again and again, helped Aidan to believe them.

Their conversations were soon interrupted by the wishes of their captain, one Oliver Hayworth. He knew they would be docking in Philadelphia in a few days. So he wanted to do what he could to present Jack and Aidan favorably to a buyer. What an amazing turn of events it was for them to see such "passionate concern" for their hygiene, appearance, health and welfare.

Jack and Aidan were ordered to spend their days topside in the fresh air and sunshine. They were fed apples, decent porridge, salted pork, fish, and freshly baked bread. And for the first time they could remember, their clothes and their bodies received the benefit of soap and water.

These changes for the better, regardless of motive, were more than welcome. Aidan and Jack's strength began to improve. And this new regimen helped take their minds away, briefly, from the terrible pain of losing their dear wife and mother.

For Jack's sake, Aidan hid his sorrow and made a conscious effort to play and laugh with his son. They received much-needed exercise by swabbing the deck, and helping with sundry chores. And despite Aidan's sorely broken heart, he began to take some fascination in how the ship was being handled.

Jack and Aidan were on deck when a call came down from the crow's nest, "Land dead ahead!" The captain stretched out a spyglass toward the horizon and pronounced, "Praise be, 'tis the mouth of the Delaware!"

"What's the Delaware?" Jack asked.

"I don't know, son, but it sounds mighty fine ta me," his father answered.

Within minutes the captain called them to his cabin.

"Mr. Smith," he addressed Aidan, "I was troubled to hear about your wife. Dreadful business, this typhus. My condolences to you."

Aidan managed to say, "Thank you."

"Yes, well, I hope you appreciate what we tried to do to soften that blow by getting you and the lad top-side and better nourished. And now that our landing in Philadelphia is imminent, let's review what is likely to happen there."

"All right," Aidan replied, as he studied the captain intently.

"You and the boy, of course, are bound for gainful employment. Your trade is always in demand on a plantation or a well-run farm.

"After the paying passengers have disembarked, we will position you on the dock where overseers representing land-owners will stroll up and down. They'll be looking to fill their needs for laborers and tradesmen. I want you both to look your very fittest.

"You must show enthusiasm and uprightness, regardless of who may approach. The boy should say nothing. And you, Smith, just speak up politely and represent your skills well. If someone is serious about purchasing your contract, a hand will fetch me and a deliberation will ensue. Do *nothing* to interfere with that. I will do my best to find you a decent situation. Is all of this understood?" the captain asked.

"Perfectly," Aidan assured him.

"Fine. Stay above deck for now, and assist the crew however you can. But be careful! Do *not* risk an injury. You are dismissed."

"What did all that mean, Papa?" Jack asked, as they made their way forward to the bow of the ship to gain the best vantage of the port ahead.

"It meant many things, Jack. But they all boil down ta this. We're goin' ta pray that God will show his great mercy upon us. We must pray that good and decent folk will agree ta provide us a place ta work and live in this new land."

"Do we get to pick 'em?" Jack wondered.

"No, son. We'll leave that up ta the Lord. Come now, let's move aft and grab our bucket."

How Aidan prayed from that moment on that a benevolent owner would employ them. He prayed for a good situation, decent tools and living conditions, edible food, agreeable people to work with, and a place where Jack would find at least a measure of the love his departed mother would have provided. Aidan also prayed that they would have a chance to somehow worship their maker.

As the ship rode swiftly on the high tide surf into the mouth of the Delaware River, Aidan and Jack hurried forward to the bow again where Jack thrilled in riding up and down as the tidal waves threw saltwater spray up over his face! Aidan held Jack tightly by the seat of the pants to keep his boy from flying right over the fore rails. But he gladly assumed that risk, for the sorely-needed fun they were having.

When the ship entered calmer waters in the channel, a strange sensation came over Aidan. This new country they'd reached was known as the land of the free. And even though their status was anything but, Aidan began to hope that, one day, they would make a fresh start of it in America.

The landing in Philadelphia seemed a lot like the waterfront on Dublin's River Liffey, except that the buildings were not as old. They favored wood and brick over stone and stucco. The bustle of activity, though, was at a similar, fevered pitch. Everywhere there were horses pulling wagons, men pushing two-wheeled carts, sailors, gentry, merchants, vendors, watchful police, and cunning dogs in search of a scrap. People laughed, cried, embraced, and waved hello or good-bye.

The well-to-do among the passenger list of *The Vigilance* disembarked first in their finery. They were delayed for only moments by customs and immigration officers. Those surviving the steerage class were held back, much like quarantined cattle. They did their best to present themselves as being fit. But their weakened bodies struggled just to regain equilibrium back on dry land. After being openly searched for disease, they were questioned about their destinations and chances of gainful employment.

After awhile, some of the crew were allowed to disembark. Crewmen lower in rank, or those being punished stayed on board with orders to sanitize the filthy lower deck. They were driven hard at this task because of an impending inspection of the ship.

Jack and Aidan ate with the crew that night, and Aidan inquired as to the date. It was the seventeenth of July, 1843.

The next morning, Jack and Aidan were ordered to take up a position on the dock where they'd be noticed. A junior ship's officer fashioned a sign: "Indentured Male, Expert Blacksmith." Below that, after questioning Aidan, he wrote in smaller letters, "Horse Shoeing, Harness Making, & Forging of Useful Objects. Inquire of Captain."

A deckhand sat with Jack and Aidan. The sailor whittled a soft pine sea serpent, while making sure his charges didn't disappear into the crowd. Jack delighted in the man's handiwork.

It did not take long before parties began to inquire of Aidan's skills. At first, the crewman acted as an agent on their behalf. But he soon deferred to Aidan directly, saying, "Just ask him."

Aidan felt nervous, considering the high stakes of what was happening. At each stranger's approach, he wondered whether this was someone he'd wish to commit his future to and Jack's welfare as well. So many times Aidan prayed, *"Lord, please just bring us the right one."*

Several individuals seemed highly interested, but were put off at the prospect of providing for Jack's needs until he could render useful service. Aidan was glad when they lost interest because he doubted, by that very objection, whether they would provide well for Jack's needs.

One merchant was specifically looking for an expert in wrought-iron gate and fence work. Aidan knew he could have mastered it, but he didn't mislead the merchant about having such experience.

Finally, an aggressive-looking man approached. He was sunken-faced, had a long gun slung over his shoulder, a pistol on each hip, and he carried a heavy riding crop that he nervously slapped on his boot top. He motioned toward Aidan with the crop as he spoke to the crewman, never addressing Aidan directly.

The stranger pressed the crewman, "Is this one healthy enough, 'ey sailor?"

"Believe so, sir, and will likely get stronger after he's been on land a bit."

"I'm an overseer from the Virginia high country. Does the boy count in the bargain?"

"His son, it is. Aye, sir, the lad comes with," affirmed the sailor.

"I'd speak with your captain, then."

The seaman replied, "Watch these two if ye please, and I'll fetch Captain Hayworth."

Aidan had a very uncomfortable feeling about this man during the few minutes that crept by while awaiting the captain's arrival. If he looked at Aidan and Jack at all, it was as if he were inspecting livestock for sale, and trying to find a defect in order to drive a better bargain.

He emitted a foul odor, as well, of roughly equal parts sweat, cheap whiskey, and chewing tobacco.

Finally the captain came and greeted the overseer.

"How do you do this fine day, sir? Captain Hayworth at your service!"

"Name's Snead," the man grumbled, rebuffing the captain's false cheer. "I represent a landed gentleman by the name of Cauley, William Lockwood Cauley, of Front Royal, Virginia. He sent me hither in search of a smith. If he's indentured, the master would require at least six years of service. What terms have you attached to this one and the lad?"

"Well, sir, your directness is admirable. Shall we pursue the particulars, as we stroll the promenade?"

"Ain't much for strolling, captain. What are your terms?"

"Mr. Snead, I have generally offered indentured contracts for terms of five to six years. But Mr. Smith's wife was to have been a part of the bargain, and she has unfortunately passed from this life during the voyage. So, perhaps we could extend the term—'

At this, Aidan could no longer hold his peace.

"She died because of the conditions on your *ship*, captain!"

Snead raised his crop at Aidan and growled, "No one asked you!"

Aidan stared directly into Snead's eyes with a look that begged this villain to strike him.

"Why, you murderer!" muttered the captain. "How dare you question me? I saved you from prison and the end of a rope!"

Snead seemed genuinely put off when he heard the crime that Aidan was charged with. "I didn't come lookin' to hire a killer!" he protested, and started to walk away.

"Good sir," soothed the captain as he took Snead by the arm, "let's do take that walk after all. I am sure the right concessions can be struck."

As they moved away a short distance, Jack asked, "Papa, why did the captain call you a murderer? What does that mean?"

"It's his wrong way of sayin' what happened ta the man back in Ireland, Jack. Don't worry. People say wrong things when they don't know the whole truth."

The captain and Snead turned about and began to approach.

"That is suitable, then, Mr. Snead? Ten years for each, Smith and the boy?"

"Not a day less, and 'tis lucky for you that I'll take 'em."

"It's settled then," replied the captain.

Aidan couldn't believe what he was hearing. They were being sold into sure abuse at the hands of this unsavory overseer, for twice the time Aidan was hoping to serve!

He thought, "*Father in heaven, what can I do? Should I grab Jack and run? Should I escape this devil once we start out? Would I have been better off in prison? Dear God, please tell me, what should I do!*"

But all Aidan could hear in a muted, almost unworldly tone, was the captain's voice saying, "Come aboard, Mr. Snead! We'll sign the necessary paperwork in my cabin and seal it with a toast to your robust health!"

# Chapter 4

As bad as being sold into servitude for ten years was for Aidan and Jack, things were about to get worse.

Snead led them two blocks to a livery, and pointed at a broken-down nag he'd purchased. He obviously was just hoping to get the journey back to Virginia out of her.

Then he barked, "Even with your attitude, Smith, you're worth more to me than the boy. That mare won't take the weight of both of you. You ride, he walks."

"A five-year-old! What chance will he have of keepin' up with men on horseback?" Aidan protested.

"You heard me."

"Then I'll walk, too," Aidan countered.

"Fine by me," Snead chuckled.

Then he fashioned a noose with a ten foot length of heavy rope.

"Just to make sure you don't take a detour into the bushes, here's a little insurance," he said, as he approached Aidan.

Snead cinched the rope around Aidan's neck and tied off the other end to the saddle on the old mare.

"Give me your satchel!" he demanded, as he snatched Aidan's bag. Though it was not much larger than a bushel, it contained all of the Smith's earthly goods. Snead roughly tied it off to the saddle as well.

"Usually, we'd just do twenty mile a day," he growled. "But since you're determined to be stubborn, we'll start out a little quicker to run the devil out of you."

Aidan swung Jack onto his shoulders, and off they sped through the narrow streets of Philadelphia. Snead, defiantly, never looked back.

Aidan's legs had not been subjected to this type of strain since long before the voyage. He wondered how long he could endure. But amazingly, after several very taxing minutes, his body began to adjust to the gait of the horses.

Then he started, in quick glances, to look about at their surroundings.

The thing that struck Aidan first was the beautiful churches, including one as large as the cathedral back home. And soon they passed the large hall of government with its tall spire. Aidan also noticed the fine house beside it.

They proceeded through an area of closely packed tradesmen's homes, all well-kept. They saw markets and later some squalor, but that gave way to countryside and an open road. Aidan was more than grateful that it was a decent road at that.

Snead sat a gelding that was squatter than the best steeds Aidan was familiar with back home. But it seemed like it might have had some of those horses bred into it. Snead's was a little chestnut mount, quick stepping, with plenty of spirit.

"The mare won't last long at this pace," Aidan shouted to Snead.

Snead turned, glanced at the older horse's frothing mouth and shouted back, "She won't or *you* won't?" The heartless fool kept right on going.

Aidan's neck and shoulders were starting to ache. While gasping for breath he said, "Jackie, boy, on this journey we're gonna pretend thou art a sweet little sack of 'taters. I'm gonna carry me sack of spuds this way now."

Then he slid Jack down to ride on his lower back and leaned forward to balance him. Later, Aidan tossed him over his shoulder so he could take relief by grabbing the saddle horn of the mare.

On they went, mile after mile, with Aidan moving the boy to and fro. Just as it seemed like Jack's weight was about to break whatever part of his father's aching body he rested on, Aidan would devise an alternate way to support his beloved son.

Then the rope became a serious problem. Aidan tried to loosen it without Snead noticing. But regardless of any short relief, the mare would pull, jostle, and re-tighten the rope. Aidan tried to keep his shirt collar under the coarse fibers to little avail. Eventually, they began to cut through his skin. His sweat flooded the open sores, causing a throbbing burn that raced all the way to his fingertips.

His only solace was that there was a rest stop every five miles to freshen horse and rider. Once, Snead sadistically delighted in speeding past a stop. But he relented and looped back to pause for his horse's benefit.

Immediately, Aidan let Jack alight. Aidan slumped over forward to help the blood flow through his back again, then arched and twisted his spine to relieve painful cramping.

At their third stop of the day, Aidan pulled two heavy work shirts out of his satchel. He tied them together to fashion a large sling. He looped it over his head to create a little seat for Jack. This device proved to give Aidan's arms some much-needed rest.

As they got underway again, Jack delighted in his new perch, and Aidan drew energy from hearing Jack giggle, and say things like, "Papa, you're my big, fast horsey!"

Jack was even able to fall asleep in the sling late in the afternoon of that first day. It was during his nap that Aidan first thought about how painfully different their circumstances were from what they had been praying for.

When they finally stopped for the night, Aidan suffered the indignity of having Snead shackle him to a post in the livery of an inn.

As Snead walked away to have a hearty dinner, Jack asked, "Papa, is *he* supposed to be the nice person you prayed God would bring, to give us a good place to live?"

That was as close as Aidan came to tears during all of their ordeal. He still hadn't had a chance to properly grieve Louisa. Exhausted, now, and fighting not to give in to despair, he was beginning to doubt the faith that had carried him thus far.

Somehow he managed to tell Jack, "Mr. Snead is a very singular man."

"What does that mean?" Jack questioned.

"It means that he puts one thing on his mind, and doesn't think about much of anythin' else."

"So what's the one thing on his mind, Papa?"

"Mr. Snead is just concerned about gettin' us back ta the place we're gonna live in Virginia, as quickly as he can. Once we're there, we'll most likely see how God has picked the right place for us."

"I hope so, Papa."

"Me too, Jackie boy."

"Papa?"

"Aye, son."

"I miss Momma."

"So do I, son," Aidan sighed.  "So do I."

# Chapter 5

The next morning, Jack and Aidan were awakened from their bed of livery straw by the agitated crow of a rooster.

The first sensations Aidan felt were the burning around his neck, and sorely throbbing feet. But within minutes, he and Jack took their usual quiet time to pray and ask for strength for the day. About half an hour later, Snead approached and unlocked the shackles.

"Eat these before we head out. You're lucky to get them," he said as he flung a few apples at their feet.

"We'll need water, too," Aidan said.

"There's water aplenty for you over there," snapped Snead, as he pointed to the horses' trough.

"We'll be too sick ta walk by noon if we drink that," Aidan countered.

"What a pity!"

Looking behind the inn, Snead motioned to a spring-house. "There, drink your fill but be quick about it."

While Aidan showed Jack how to cup his hands to drink from a pipe spilling clean, cool water out of the base of the springhouse, a maid came from within where she'd gone to fetch supplies for the kitchen. From their desperate appearance, she quickly sensed Jack and Aidan's horrible plight and took pity on them.

She slipped Aidan a wonderful round of cheese from her apron and whispered, "Here, sir. God bless you both."

"Thank ye. Thank ye and bless thee, miss!" Aidan said in grateful disbelief. "By the way, miss," he continued, "what is the name of this place?"

"You're just outside Wilmington, sir."

"Wilmington?"

Hearing Aidan's thick Irish accent, she clarified, "That's Wilmington, Delaware." Then she quickly returned to the springhouse to replace the cheese.

It would have been far beyond Aidan's decent command of language to explain how much having that smuggled food meant to them. Right off, Jack went from being Aidan's little sack of taters, to a whisker-wiggling mouse.

Snead must have thought them daft, but he wasn't curious enough to stop and demand to know what they were playing at. He occasionally looked back at their mirth, but just shook his head in ridicule and pressed on.

Aidan used the rest stops that day to wrap his feet with cool, wet rags. He grew concerned whether his boots would survive the whole journey, and he prayed they'd hold up.

Once again, Jack was able to sleep some in the late afternoon. But Aidan was hurting and being pushed beyond exhaustion.

Then another fortunate thing happened that second day. It came at the expense of Snead's horse when it started to favor its left front hoof. There was obviously something wrong with its front right.

"Your horse is limpin'!" Aidan cautioned Snead.

"Probably just a stone under the shoe," he said with indifference.

When he decided to be obstinate, Snead was immovable. The next rest stop was at least three miles on. By the time they got there, the horse's condition had become serious.

Snead dismounted and snarled, "You're the horse expert. *Look* at it!" as he headed out back to relieve himself.

Aidan soothed the animal, then gently lifted its throbbing foot, which was already caked with dried blood. The poor animal had stepped on a rusty spike that penetrated deep inside the hoof.

"Steady, boy, "Aidan whispered as he gave a quick, hard pull on the nail head.

The horse whinnied, but didn't bolt.

"What did you find?" demanded Snead as he swaggered back.

Aidan turned and presented the bloody nail.

"At least that explains it," Snead said coldly.

"The wound will need cleaning, or—"

"Or what, smith? He'll limp a bit? All the better for you. Put that rope back around your neck."

"I'm telling you, man, this horse can get lockjaw, even die from that rusty nail."

Snead ignored Aidan and led the horse to the trough for a drink. Then he mounted, and dragged them onward.

As Aidan grimaced at the gelding's painful gait he wondered, *"What makes a man that uncaring and cruel?"*

It was inevitable that the horse got worse. Finally, Snead had to dismount.

"What's needed to dress the wound, Smith?"

Aidan asked, "Do ye have any whiskey ta clean it with?"

Snead produced a half-empty pint from his saddlebag.

"What else, smith?"

"If he were in my stable, I'd cover the bottom of that hoof for two days to keep it clean."

"We've got too many miles to go for that. Give me an idea that will work!"

"Do ye have a candle?" Aidan asked.

Snead produced one.

"And a match, and an apple?"

"An apple?" Snead protested.

"Ta distract the horse," Aidan replied.

Aidan cleaned the hoof with the whiskey while the gelding munched away. Then he melted some candle wax to seal the wound. The horse barely flinched during the treatment.

"I'd switch to the mare if I were you," Aidan told Snead.

"I intended to," he claimed.

Within minutes they were moving again, but at a much slower pace. It had pained Aidan to see Snead's horse suffering. But he was so very glad that he didn't have to run anymore.

# Chapter 6

Baltimore was the second real American city that Jack and Aidan saw. It seemed to be large, and growing by the day.

They had time to learn some things about Baltimore. Snead took the stop there as his opportunity to do the town before they made an important rendezvous two days later in the country's new capital, Washington City.

The livery that was Aidan and Jack's home for the next twenty hours, was run by a freed black man by the name of Roebuck Chandler. Roebuck had learned the blacksmith's trade as a youth on a tobacco plantation in North Carolina. He described his master there as, "A good, young man more disposed to kindness than his father was." He'd allowed Roebuck to hire out to do work for others. Then Roebuck and his young master equally split the proceeds.

Roebuck proudly stated, "After twenty long year o' thrift an' hard work, I was able ta buy my own *freedom*! Then I come north ta work, hopin' for a better life."

"Hopin'?" Aidan asked.

"Tha's right. Some days, I ain't sure I come north far enough."

Roebuck knew something of the Virginia Valley where Jack and Aidan were headed. He said that much of the grain it produced wound up moving through the port of Baltimore, and then was shipped around the world. He mentioned that considerable beef and other livestock were raised in the valley as well.

Aidan and Jack's new acquaintance had only a passing knowledge of Snead. He recalled seeing him a time or two before, and that Snead seemed to be "the kind o' man that regard free blacks with a particular dislike."

As they prepared to leave for Washington the next day, Jack and Aidan felt a touch of sadness. The kitchen maid in Wilmington had shown them kindness. But Roebuck Chandler was the first real friend they'd made in America.

Snead burst out a side door of the inn about two hours later than their usual start time and staggered down the path toward them. That was the first time Aidan had seen Snead hung over from drink.

"Smith!" he snarled. "Them horses ready?"

"As ready as they can be," Aidan evenly replied.

"You'd damn well better be ready, too. We've lost time somewhares this morning, and we're about to make up for it!" he bellowed.

Snead brutalized them and the horses that morning. But his evil energy soon waned as the sun rose higher and began to beat down upon him. They started to slow, and it was then that Aidan gave Jack permission to pull out the little toy Roebuck had made for him. He'd fashioned a wooden ball on a string, attached to a handle crowned with a small cup. Jack spent hours mastering just the right timing to swing the ball up and into the cup while bouncing on his father's back.

On their way out of town, they saw huge, wooden grain silos standing like massive monuments against the bright blue sky.

Before long, they saw a waterway running parallel to the road. Jack yelled out, "Look, Papa, it's a boat!"

"That's a barge," corrected Snead. "Canal connects Baltimore, the capital at Washington City, and Pittsburgh up in Pennsylvania."

Aidan thought that the barge looked similar to the boats on the Irish Grand Canal. A family sat upon the roof as a pair of dusty mules pulled the barge from a towpath to the right. The waterway was about twenty-five feet across. There was a towpath on the other side, too, serving opposing traffic. How genteel those fine folk looked, gliding easily along as Snead and his weary charges trudged past them.

When the condition of the road worsened, Snead cut through a section of light brush to take up on the canal path for awhile. When they had to slow after catching up to a mule team, they crossed back to the road, which had improved at that point.

It was hot. But their closeness to the water, a bit of breeze and nearby shade trees made the weather slightly more bearable. Snead stopped at a roadside fruit vendor about midday. He surprised Aidan by buying a small, ripe watermelon for them. Again, Snead rolled the fruit to their feet like he was feeding animals. But how sweet that melon tasted! It was definitely the high point of that section of the journey which wound down at about two o'clock the following afternoon, as they entered the outskirts of Washington City.

Although Snead proceeded to skirt the center of Washington, Jack and Aidan could see impressive sites in the distance. To Aidan's eye, the developing capital had a definite grandeur about it. There were wide boulevards and prominent buildings, like the White House and the huge capital building with its green, copper dome. Jack was in awe of these new surroundings.

Aidan figured it took about three quarters of an hour to maneuver around Washington before they reached a large roadside inn. His instincts placed them somewhere on the western outskirts of the city.

Snead tied off the horses and was about to tell Aidan to take the rope off his neck, when a lady called out Snead's name in rage.

"Mr. Snead! What have you *done* to that man?" she cried.

Jack and Aidan turned to behold Mrs. Isabel Cauley for the first time. She came bustling toward them accompanied by her maid. Although slight of build, and endowed with a girlish beauty, Mrs. Cauley had a determination of purpose that announced she was not to be trifled with.

"How *dare* you treat a human being like this! Get that rope off him immediately!" she berated Snead.

Mrs. Cauley approached Aidan and was shocked to see the raw, festering rope burn around his neck. Aidan flushed with embarrassment as she had to raise her perfumed handkerchief to her nose as she came close enough to him to inspect his wounds.

She stepped back slightly, lowered her handkerchief and pleasantly asked, "Are you the new blacksmith?"

"Why, yes, madam, I am. Aidan Smith, your humble servant. And this is me son, Jack."

Mrs. Cauley was nearly reduced to tears at their pathetic appearance, but she steadied herself to say, "Well, I am most glad to make your acquaintances."

To that, Snead emitted a sound of disgust.

"Snead!" she demanded. "Why have they not traveled on horseback all this way?"

"Gave the father that choice right off, in Philadelphia, ma'am."

"The father only and not the boy?"

"Believe so, ma'am," Snead mumbled.

"Why, that's outrageous! You expected a lad so tiny to walk? He's a child, for heaven's sake! They'll not walk another step on this journey. Mr. Smith, you'll join Essex on the driver's seat," she said, pointing to her coachman in the distance. "And young Jack," she added tenderly, "you'll join Liza and me inside the coach—as soon as we've scrubbed you a bit. Liza, gather a set of the new play clothes I purchased for Jonathan, and towels and soap from the inn."

In no time, Mrs. Cauley and her maid brought Jack back from behind the springhouse looking a regular little prince.

Then Liza looked after Aidan's neck wounds.

"Doesn't that burn, the soap and water?" she asked as she gently patted a wet cloth against Aidan's encrusted skin.

"Not as bad as hot iron when ye grab it by mistake." Aidan said with a light chuckle.

"Oh?" Liza said, as Aidan turned his palms upward for her to inspect. As she did, he glanced at her face. It seemed to him to be both strong and fine. And her skin was a rich, smooth brown.

"Um, I see a scar or two on those hands," Liza acknowledged. "Of course, I don't suppose you'd be much of a blacksmith without them," she offered.

"I'm Aidan."

"I see."

"And you are, miss?"

"Oh, pardon me, Mr. Smith."

"Aidan."

"All right, *Aidan*. I'm Liza Moore, Ms. Isabel's personal maid."

"That means house niggah," scoffed Snead as he swaggered by and spit tobacco juice at their feet.

Aidan just scowled after him for a moment.

Turning back toward them, Snead said, "And you'd best watch this one, Miss Liza. He's killed a man. Good thing for him there wasn't another blacksmith on the dock."

Then Snead strolled away as if he'd delivered Aidan a deathblow.

Completely ignoring his comment, Liza asked, "Aidan, do you have a clean shirt to put on?"

Amazed at her total indifference to Snead's comment, he softly asked, "Don't ye want ta know about what Snead just said?"

"Not unless you want to tell me. Now, I don't want that wound to fester, so we best keep it clean. I'll ask inside for some cloth to cut into bandages."

Aidan's terrible deed in Ireland always loomed in his mind as a dark secret he hoped no one would learn. He was amazed, and pleased that Liza seemed set on making up her own mind about him.

Then Mrs. Cauley insisted they eat and drink. Within minutes, Liza produced not only clean cotton bandages for Aidan, but also an entire outdoor picnic from the inn's kitchen. There was freshly-roasted chicken, potato salad, boiled greens and biscuits. They even had tasty, fresh cider to refresh them.

Aidan was so hungry for their feast that, right after Mrs. Cauley offered grace, he began eating more like a starved animal than a grateful man. When he caught sight of the mistress looking pitifully at him, he felt the same way he had when she'd raised her handkerchief to approach him.

But soon fed, scrubbed, wounds treated, and rested, Jack and Aidan took up their greatly improved positions upon and within the Cauley's splendid coach.

# Chapter 7

After enjoying Mrs. Cauley's picnic, sitting beside Essex on the softly-sprung driver's seat was Aidan's second real joy in her employ. Essex handled a beautiful team of dapple gray carriage horses with ease. It was obvious how comfortable they were with him.

Snead was left to follow behind.

Almost immediately, giggling spilled from inside the coach. It prompted Aidan, against his nature, to eavesdrop.

"Well, Jack," exclaimed Mrs. Cauley, "why don't we have a little talk and get to know one another?"

"I'd like that. But . . ." Jack hesitated.

"But what?" she asked curiously.

"Could you please tell me, ma'am, what I'm supposed to call you?"

"You just call me Mrs. Isabel," the mistress replied.

With a front tooth missing, Jack's version of her name came out something like "Mith Ithabel."

"And you, ma'am?" he directed to Liza.

"Why, I'm Miss Liza, Jack."

There was silence as Jack considered something.

"Can I ask you a question, Mith Liza?"

"About why I look different?" she guessed.

"You're real pretty and everything. But I never saw somebody like you, except where we got off the boat, and when we met Roebuck."

"Roebuck?" Liza asked.

"He's our friend. He's a blacksmith in Baltimore."

"Oh, I see. Well, Roebuck and I look different from you because, long ago, our people came across the ocean from a place called Africa."

"Does everyone look like you there?"

"Pretty much."

"Well . . . I think you look real nice, just—"

"Different," Liza kindly completed his thought.

Mrs. Cauley said, "And you came to us across the great ocean, too, didn't you Jack?"

"Oh, yes, ma'am," he replied with gravity.

"I'm sure it was a difficult journey," she continued. "But tell us about where you came from. What do you like about it there, Jack?"

"It's real pretty and green. We live in Kilkenny."

"Why, that sounds like a charming place."

"Papa says it's just a right old Irish name. That's what we are, we're Irish."

"And that's a wonderful thing to be. You can be proud of being Irish, Jack," Mrs. Cauley added. "And what about your mother? Did she stay behind in Ireland?"

Jack must have begun to sob, then. Aidan couldn't make out what Jack said next, but he heard the women trying to comfort him. They told him it was all right not to talk about it. But eventually, he did.

"She was the best momma ever, in the whole, wide world. All she did was think about us and everybody else. She even gave away most all of her own food on the boat. Papa says that's maybe why she got sick and died with my little brother or sister inside of her."

Now the women were sobbing, too. They hugged Jack and comforted him.

For some time, then, the coach rocked on in silence.

# Chapter 8

"Essex, what is the name of the place we're headed for?" Aidan asked.

"Plantation called High Meadows. Dat's what we is, beautiful meadows way up a mountain valley," he said with pride.

"Um, and how long have you been there?"

"Born and raised. I'm thirty year old."

"You handle a team well," Aidan observed.

"Dem two's Ms. Isabel's pride and joy," Essex said. Then he leaned toward Aidan and whispered, "She a fine Christian woman, mind. But I can tell Ms. Isabel have a dose o' worldly pride 'bout dese here animals. Me too. Takes care of Luke and Henry like dey's my own."

"I can see that from their condition. And they look to be no more than six years old?" Aidan estimated.

"You good, mistah. Luke six. Henry from de same sire. He five."

"Call me Aidan."

"All right, den, Aidan. Where you from?"

"Kilkenny, Ireland."

"Ain't exactly heard of it, but sound like it could be a long ways from here."

"Indeed. We came a long way and at a great cost. I lost me wife on the sea crossin' ta typhus. The boy's all I've got now."

"Sorry 'bout your missus. I mean it . . . but de boy . . . Ms. Isabel takin' a shine ta him already," smiled Essex.

"Yes, I'm grateful. I'm a smith. What happened to the one you had at High Meadows before me?"

"De blacksmith? Whiskey took him. Dey say ol' Dawson's liver give out. Weren't worth much de' las' couple years anyways, him bein' drunk an' sick mos' de time. Guess he were all right when he was young. I always shoed dese here horses myself."

"Did he have a family?"

"Wife lef' him long ago. But he seem happy ta jus' stay on wit' us an' do little as he could get away with. Plus, ever-body in de valley knows, Cauleys is de bes' folk ta work for. Dat is," Essex whispered, "less you get on de wrong side o' Snead."

Essex glanced at the bandages on Aidan's neck. "You comin' here a free man, Mr. Aidan?"

"No. I'm an indentured servant. So is Jack."

"Um. Ain't heard of indentured servants 'round home since I was a boy. Sho' didn't want ta be one back den."

"Why's that?"

"Cause you ain't a slave, so you ain't de *property* o' de mastah. It mo' like he jus' rentin' ya fo' a time. So some o' dem ol' mastahs figures ta whip ya like a rented mule, 'specially when time get close fo' settin' ya free again. Dey wants ta get ever las' drop o' work out ya."

Essex's comments made Aidan shift a bit.

Essex glanced back at Snead and said, "But I don't *think* ya has ta worry 'bout dat, workin' at High Meadows. Cause you workin' fo' William Lockwood Cauley!" he said with an air of pride at the grand-sounding name of the man who owned him. "You won't see him much, though."

"Why is that?" Aidan asked.

"'Count o' he all de time doin' somethin' fo' de great Commonwealth o' Virginia. Mos' times, Ms. Isabel say he be in Richmond, to de House o' Delegates. But some time he off ta Washington City, or even Philadelphia or New York. Our master one, important gen'leman!"

"He treats you well?"

"He a fine Christian man—*real* Christian, not one o' dem 'goes ta church Sundays, whips my niggahs Mondays kind o' man. But like I said, it ain't de mastah you has ta worry 'bout. It," lowering his voice, "Phineas T. Snead."

Aidan chuckled at hearing Snead's full name for the first time.

"But Essex," Aidan whispered, "if the Cauleys are known for their kindness, why did they hire him?"

"Like I said, master away mos' de time. He know ol' Snead will keep order, and keep de mistress safe. Even half sober, he de best shot in all de county. And when he sell crops, ain't a man alive gwan cheat him."

"I see," Aidan said, still not completely sure why a man like Snead would be employed by someone as noble as his new mistress and her husband.

Then Essex said, "If ya don't mind me askin', Mr. Aidan, why is it dat you *owes* servitude?"

"In part, ta pay for our ship passage."

"Um, dat would be a sum o' money."

Aidan was beginning to feel at ease with Essex. And emboldened by Liza's apparent acceptance of him, he risked saying, "And I was in trouble with the law."

"You, Mr. Aidan?"

"A drunken sot tried ta molest me wife while I was callin' for a carriage. So I hit him."

"He deserve it, den."

"Yes, but he died."

"Oh, Lawd!"

"And he was a nobleman."

"Wha's dat?"

"I guess you'd say it's kind of like a master."

"Now I seein' why you in servitude!"

"I wish I'd never thrown that punch, Essex."

"Well, even though y'all from far away, sound like it ain't dat much different from de kind o' troubles we has here."

Aidan overheard Jack asking, "Mith Ithabel, do you have a boy these new clothes are for?"

"I have a grandson, Jonathan, whom I bought them for. But they are yours to keep now, Jack. He surely won't mind. Jonathan has plenty of clothes."

"Is he nice, your grandson?"

"I like to think so," said Mrs. Cauley.

"He's a right, little gentleman," offered Miss Liza.

"Will I get to play with him?" wondered Jack.

Aidan felt uneasy about Jack's question. But in her ever-gracious way, Mrs. Cauley quickly said, "Of course, Jack. Jonathan will be free to visit and play with you as much as possible. He lives not so very far from us."

Comforted by that news, Jack boasted, "My Papa's a smith. Did you know that?"

"I believe I did hear that," said Mrs. Cauley.

"He can make you anything from iron, even toys or a hook to hang your hat on. Is there some work you want me to do, too, Mith Ithabel?"

Liza asked, "What kind of work are you good at, Jack?"

"I'm a pretty good picker upper. Papa taught me how to use a broom, too."

"Well," the mistress assured Jack with a smile, "that's going to come in very handy at a place as big and busy as High Meadows."

# Chapter 9

It took two days by carriage to travel from Washington City to Aidan and Jack's new home.

Along the way, Aidan was curious to watch how Mrs. Cauley treated Snead. She seemed to settle into an icy tolerance of the man.

Jack completely charmed his two female companions. They treated him kindly, and were careful not to pry too deeply into his family's affairs through Jack's innocent mind.

Essex was a fine traveling companion, too.

"Mind if I sings a little, Mr. Aidan?"

"I'd welcome it, Essex, I'm sure."

"Is you a singin' man youself?" Essex asked.

"Of course. I'm Irish! We all sing—and better than the Welsh, I might add."

"Da's good, cause our kind o' singin' take mo' dan jus' one, ta do it right. I'll start, an' you join in whenever you feels like it. All right?"

"I'll give it a try, Essex."

"Dis here a little song I been workin' on ta tell how I got faith in Jesus."

"I'd love to hear it!"

"Good. Jus' has de firs' part down. Go like dis. Oh, ohhh, ohh, ohh, ohhh, I-I was, broken an' hurt—now your turn."

Aidan hesitated, but then followed with, "I was hurt."

"Hey, you singin' voice pretty good!" Essex continued, "I was drownin' in my sin."

Aidan sang, "In my sin."

"When I felt someone's touch,"

"Someone's touch."

"Turned around an' saw him."

"I saw him!" Aidan finished.

"You *are* good, Mr. Aidan! Comin' in right on time."

"You're good, too, Essex. I like the message and the beat of your song. Let's do it a couple more times."

"We has a lot o' ridin' lef'. We can sing it a hundred time, Mr. Aidan!"

Essex leaned back and sang the first verse again with joy and conviction. Aidan joined him to the apparent delight of the coach's occupants.

Leaning her head outside, Liza teased, "I thought you were a workin' man, Mr. Aidan, not some travelin', singin' kind o' man!"

"Not me, Miss Liza. I'm just tryin' ta keep up with Essex here."

"He better'n me!" shouted Essex.

"Thanks. I need a little encouragin'," Aidan replied.

"I don't think so!" Liza laughed, then retreated inside.

"OK, Essex, what comes next?" Aidan asked.

"Well, I know what I wants ta say. In de firs' part, I'm sayin' how it seem like Jesus jus' come up from behind me one day, an' tap me on de shoulder. You know, in a manner o' speakin'."

"OK, good. Then what?"

"Well, instead of me bein' all scared an' tremblin' when Jesus got hold o' me, it were mo' like he jus' sayin' everthin' gwan be all right. It weren't like I had ta *do* somethin' ta get all holy right away. I jus' tol' him I's a sinner, an ast him forgive me. Den, he took away all de troublement from offa' my mind. And it were jus' like he standin' right dere, smilin', like we's friends."

"Um...that sounds like scripture."

"Oh, you know de book pretty good, den."

Essex and Aidan worked at creating the song word by word, phrase by phrase, and line by line. It was such a joy for Aidan to get to know Essex and his faith this way.

At a rest stop Aidan asked, "What do you want the song's chorus ta say?"

"What's a chorus?"

"That's the part that carries a main idea you want people ta know or learn about. What we've been workin' on so far are the verses. They tell the *story* of the song. Then the chorus comes along and gives people the *message* you want to give them. After that, more verses come ta tell the story, then—"

"Den de chorus come on again?" asked Essex.

"That's right, to plant the message more deeply."

"Yeah, slaves got some songs like dat, Mr. Aidan."

"Good. I'd like to learn them! So, what is the main idea you want *your* chorus ta say?

"Well, after sayin' dat de Lawd come *to* me, I wants ta say how he de mos' powerful God, on account of he can do anythin' he *want*. But he can be de mos' gentle God, too, all at de same time!"

"You really do know him, Essex. He has the power to defeat any enemy, but the Word tells us he'll ne'er break a tender reed."

"Can you *read* de Bible, Mr. Aidan?"

"Read it every day."

"Seem like you a preacher man!"

"Not really, Essex. I don't have the true book learnin' for that. But I do like ta share what the Word teaches."

"Den somethin' else I'm wonderin' 'bout."

"What is it, Essex?"

"How you learn ta read, you bein' a workin' man an' all?"

"My mother was a schoolmarm. And I'm lucky, too, that she led the church choir."

"Choir?"

"The singin'."

"Well, dat's good enough fo' me, Mr. Aidan."

"Good enough?"

Whispering again, Essex said, "Ya see, we don't like de preacher mastah bring us. Ol' Mr. Steadman only beat one drum—'slaves, obey you mastah.' Gots ta be mo' in de book dan jus' dat."

"There is, Essex. There's much more."

"All right, den. Far's I'm concerned, you our new preacher!"

# Chapter 10

It has been said that if you truly love someone, you'll want to share all that is beautiful with them.

On the second day's ride out of Washington, Aidan could see something looming ahead that struck a strong chord in his heart—the Blue Ridge Mountains! He stifled the still-present instinct to call out to Louisa.

"Jack!" Aidan cried. "Look what's up ahead!"

Jack had fallen asleep on Miss Liza's lap. She poked her head out of the coach. "He's sleeping like a baby," she whispered to Aidan, just loudly enough to be heard above the clop and jingle of hoof and harness.

Liza's pleasant expression changed to concern as she glanced at the discolored bandages on Aidan's neck. She withdrew for a moment, then popped her head out again and yelled, "Essex, best pull over!"

"Water hole up yonder, Miss Liza. I'll stop there."

When Aidan got down from the driver's seat to lead the team to the water, Liza hopped out of the coach and scurried toward him.

"Mr. Aidan, let me tend to your neck while we're stopped."

Then she surveyed the watering hole, and spied fresh spring water spilling from a cistern pipe, jutting from the hillside above.

"Let's go up there where the water is pure," she said.

As he followed her, Aidan thought it odd to see a woman so well-dressed, with petticoats rustling, making her way around the muddy edge of a wilderness pond.

"I'll go first, Miss Liza," he said, as he overtook her and began trampling loud enough to frighten away any creeping thing that might be underfoot.

The water stream made a steady, penetrating sound as it arched from the cistern pipe and plunged into the cool, green pond below. The area was shaded, and a pleasant breeze blew. Aidan rinsed out a tin cup that sat on the cistern capstone, filled it with a drink of fresh water and handed it to Liza.

"I'm supposed to be caring for you!" she protested.

"You are, Miss Liza, just by your kindness ta me. And I want ta thank ye for somethin' else."

Puzzled, she asked, "What's that?"

"For bein' so kind ta Jack."

"Oh, he's such a sweet child."

"Thank ye. But he's also one that's been deeply hurt."

"I know he misses his momma."

"Yes," Aidan sighed.

"And I imagine you miss her, too."

Aidan just looked down. He was caught off guard by Liza's directness, and was not at a point in losing Louisa that he could easily speak of her.

Liza produced a soft kerchief from her pocket and soaked it in the spring water. Then she gently pressed it around the open wounds on Aidan's neck.

"I have a little more of the mistress's face creme that we can put on, Mr. Aidan. But you're going to need to see Auntie Dee as soon as we reach High Meadows."

"Auntie Dee?" he asked.

Liza giggled, which made Aidan look confused.

"I'm sorry. I'm not laughing *at* you," she explained. "It's just hard to imagine anyone who doesn't already know Auntie Dee. But you will," Liza said with assurance.

"I see. And Auntie Dee will treat me neck?"

"That, and anything else that ails you!"

# Chapter 11

What a glorious sight the Virginia Valley is—fine, fertile land. On its eastern edge, the Blue Ridge Mountains mark the valley's boundary. They give way to miles of rich farmland, bordered on the far west by the Appalachian Mountain Range.

Here and there, a smaller ridge rises up from the plain between the two great chains. Such is the case with the Massanutten Mountains that marked the end of the party's journey to High Meadows.

When they saw the Massanuttens in the distance, Essex told Aidan, "Dey's a story 'bout why dey call de mountains Massanutten. Don't know if it true or not, Mr. Aidan. But folks claims a slave boy was caught up dere wit' a loaf o' bread he stole. He were hidin' it behind his back when de mastah come by an' say ta him, 'Boy, what you got behind you back?' De scared boy jus' say, 'Massa, nuttin'!' So dat's how dem mountains s'posed ta get de name!"

Aidan laughed, and never forgot "Massanutten."

As the horses began to strain at the increasing grade, something occurred that helped explain why Mrs. Cauley included Snead on her journeys. When the road began to narrow in the foothills, travelers encountered blind twists and turns, and overhanging limbs.

Suddenly, two riders swung around a bend toward the carriage. The coach horses startled and reared. As Aidan leaped down to steady them, the two strangers looked like they could mean the Cauley party harm. But Snead quickly drew a handgun on each of them.

The larger of the two men cried out, "Nothin' ta get excited about, mister! We just took that bend a might quick. Let us by, and we'll be on our way."

Mrs. Cauley observed these proceedings from the side of the carriage. She seemed to be memorizing every detail of the strangers' appearance as they hurried past her and doffed their hats.

Then she looked at her overseer and calmly said, "Well done, Mr. Snead. Carry on, Essex."

As Aidan took his seat again beside him, Essex said, "Don't be surprised, Mr. Aidan. Dis part o' de journey famous fo' no accounts tryin' ta pocket travelers' money. Ol' Snead liked ta treat hisself ta some target practice. Glad he didn't. You an' me'd end up diggin' graves, an' dis here ground ain't nothin' but limestone."

After the excitement, Jack joined the men up front. Perched between them, he began yawning and rubbing his ears.

"Papa, my ears feel like they're all clogged up."

Essex said, "Swallow hard an' your ears'll pop, son. Happen cause we gettin' up ta higher groun'."

Just then, Aidan's popped, too. That had never happened to him before.

It was the beginning of countless new things Jack and Aidan would have to get used to. And just like the new company they were keeping, they'd learn to take the bad with the good.

# Chapter 12

"Lawd, dey back!" cried Auntie Dee in a jubilant, echoing voice as the carriage approached the manse at High Meadows. What a sight Auntie Dee was! A substantial woman in her late-forties, her smooth, broad face radiated the joy of a mother discovering a lost child.

"Hurry, Essex! Get dat fancy wagon parked unduh dis here shade tree fuh Ms. Isabel. Hello, Ms. Isabel! Hello, Liza!" Auntie Dee cried.

Dogs barked, field hands waved and shouted, the rooster crowed, and a joyful, general commotion continued for the next ten minutes. Auntie Dee shouted at people seen and unseen. Mrs. Cauley's family bound out of the beautiful manse and raced out on the lawn to greet her. Her son, William, reached the carriage first.

"Mother, it's good to have you back with us!" he said, as he warmly embraced her.

"William! Thank you for keeping an eye on the place. Everything all right?"

"Fine, and you have a strong, new colt to see later."

"Wonderful!"

Next, a little boy arrived all out of breath. Jonathan, whose clothes Jack was wearing cried, "Grandma, I missed you!"

Mrs. Cauley swept him up in her arms.

"Good heavens, I don't know exactly what it is about this young man that makes me miss him so!"

"Mother Cauley, so nice to see you," offered William's wife, Caroline, as the two women embraced around Jonathan.

"It is good to see you again, dear. I thought of you so often."

Auntie Dee couldn't wait any longer.

"Now daggone, Ms. Isabel, was all I could do ta keep dis place a-runnin' wit'out yuh," bubbled Auntie Dee as she hugged her mistress.

Other slaves waved and called greetings from the manse windows.

"Well, my goodness!" cried Mrs. Cauley, as if gasping for air. "I appreciate all of you greeting us so warmly! And it was worthwhile to make our journey, because two new people have come to live and work with us at High Meadows," she said, while gracefully motioning toward Jack and Aidan.

Aidan grabbed Jack and swung him onto his shoulders.

"This is Mr. Aidan Smith and his son, Jack," the mistress continued. "Mr. Aidan is our new blacksmith."

It seemed like everyone chimed in with some sort of greeting at Mrs. Cauley's announcement.

"It's a party!" Jack exclaimed.

Seeing all of this love did both Aidan and Jack good, until Snead asserted himself.

"Follow me to your quarters!" he demanded.

Miss Liza observed what was happening and whispered to Aidan, "I'll come take you to Auntie Dee, once you get settled."

# Chapter 13

When Essex told Aidan of the troubles the smith before him had suffered, it helped prepare Aidan for his first sight of the quarters he and Jack and would live in.

"Papa, is this a place for people, or for pigs?" Jack asked within full hearing of Mr. Snead.

"Humph," Snead snorted. "It's better than some have here. Get to setting this place right. Wakeup bell sounds at five fifteen. You'll be expected to commence work by six. Start by tending that lame horse."

"What about food?" Aidan asked.

"Ask the other slaves. Maybe they'll give you something."

Jack looked sullen as Snead swaggered away with his words "the other slaves" still hanging in the air.

To lighten the mood, Aidan said, "Hey, Jack be nimble! I want ta tell ye a very special secret!"

"What, Papa?"

"If you'll help your papa, we're gonna fix this place up so smartly, that the new friends we're makin' will like it here. They'll want ta come see us, whenever they can."

"Just like at the forge back home?"

"Exactly so! But y'know what we need ta be doin' first?"

"Pray, Papa?"

"That's right. Would ye be ready ta lead our prayer then?"

"Sure, Papa," said Jack, as they quickly bowed their heads.

"Dear Heavenly Father, please help us get this horrible place so we can live in it and have our friends, like Mith Liza and Mr. Essex and that boy Jonathan come here. And God, please help me and Papa do our work good and make Mith Ithabel happy we came here."

Aidan was welling with pride, and thought Jack had finished when the boy added, "And help me and Papa not miss Momma so much. We know you're taking good care of her for us. Amen."

Aidan was still hugging and rocking Jack on his lap when they heard a rapid footfall on the gravel path.

"Mith Liza!" Jack squealed as he ran to greet her.

"Master Jack!" she returned as she reached warmly for the boy as she came in.

"Miss Liza," Aidan said with surprise. "Thank you for coming so soon. You couldn't have even unpacked yet."

"Plenty of time for that. You must have some questions."

"Yes. Do you know where we're to sleep?"

"I think Dawson slept back through that door," Liza pointed.

As they all entered a kind of lean-to attached to the forge, the stench reminded Aidan of being on the ship.

"Lord," cried Liza. "This isn't fit for a beast to sleep in. Give me three minutes to fetch two buckets of lye water, and we'll scrub this place top to bottom. Then we'll go see Auntie Dee."

# Chapter 14

Aidan was full of anticipation to meet Auntie Dee. She didn't disappoint. Auntie lived and worked in a detached kitchen, set back on an angle, twenty paces from the manse's back door.

"Hello, Mr. Aidan. An' dis young man mus' be Jack! Come here, chile, let Auntie Dee take a look at dat handsome head o' curly hair. My, my, my. How yuh be, son?"

"Very well, Miss Auntie."

"Miss Auntie? Ain't heard dat one befuh'! Yuh jus' call me Auntie Dee. Now," she said, as if trying to recall some monumental fact, "can I 'member, if I baked sumpin' good tuhday, dat a young boy wuh like ta eat? Le' me see," she said as she placed one hand on her hip while tapping an index finger to her lips. "Ah!" she cried. "Jackie, fetch me dat big jar sittin' yonder, an' make fuh quick about it!"

Jack retrieved a large crock with a lid from a shelf in the corner.

"Here you are, Auntie Dee!" he said, as he strained to lift the jar to her.

She took it and said, "Now take off de lid an' reach yuh down in."

Jack reached up, then down into the jar without being able to see the contents. When he retrieved one of Auntie Dee's big molasses cookies, his eyes brightened.

"This looks good, Auntie Dee. Thank you!"

"Well, bes' try it fus', so's yuh can make shuh!"

Jack delighted in polishing off the first of several moist, chewy cookies that were the only sugary treats he'd had in months. Before long they were all seated, enjoying cookies and a fine cup of tea made with a blend that Mrs. Cauley had given Auntie Dee at Christmas. After a few minutes of polite chatter, Auntie could no longer help herself.

"Jackie boy," she said, patting her lap, "come on obuh ta me, chile, an' sit. I reckon yuh needs a li'l Auntieizin'!"

The sight of Jack looking so content and secure in the warm, abundant embrace of this godly woman, was an answer to Aidan's prayers.

After awhile, Miss Liza took over occupying Jack, as Auntie Dee tended to Aidan's neck wounds.

"Mr. Aidan," she said as she produced a bottle from a cupboard and removed the cork, "does yuh wants ta drink some o' dis here corn liquor, befuh I treats yuh neck wit' it?"

Aidan said, "Auntie Dee, I doubt many Irishmen would say this, but no thank you. Go ahead and clean the wound."

As her skillful hands tended to Aidan, he calmly endured the burning pain from the whiskey as he asked her, "How did you come to be called Auntie Dee?"

"Well, Mr. Aidan, da's jus' what dey calls me. Got me a real name d'ough. In fact, got me two. Fus' name Daliah. Now da's my Christian name. My family name be Anderson. Tell de actual trut', ain't nebuh been all dat fond o' my Christian name, cause peoples wants ta call me Deelia, or Delilah, or some such. So suit me jus' fine if dey calls me Auntie Dee. An' fuh de mos' part, da's what I ends up bein', jus' like dey Auntie."

"Have you lived here all your life, Auntie Dee?"

"Wish ta heavens I did!"

That made Aidan even more interested as he asked, "Would you tell me about your life where you came from?"

"Well, Mr. Aidan, I can do dat in jus' one word—*Gullah!* Da's right. An' dat ain't no *place* now. Da's what we calls a way of life down de lowlands."

"The lowlands?"

"Mm-hmm. De lowlands is dem sea islands offa' Sou' Cuhlinah an' Geeohhjah. Gullahs down dere all slabes belongin' ta rice planters. We hard workin' an' hard lovin' as dey let us be."

"And you were born there?"

"Um hmm. I can remember when I were jus' a chile. I hears old-timers talkin' 'bout where we comes from, 'cross de sea. We comes from place call Sierra Leone. Da's Africa. Don't know much 'bout it myself, 'cept what I seen in de ways old-timers carryin' on. Say all what come acrost from dere hab a 'S' brand, right on dey breas'."

"A brand? That's barbaric!"

"I knows! But dey done wors'n dat to us, Mr. Aidan. Don't matter. We stays tugedduh, us Gullah. We cooks our way, laughs our way, loves our way, an' sings our way. Iz a good way—de Gullah way! An' we done all dat in plenty hard time, much worse'n what we got up here."

"You like it better here?" Aidan asked.

"Likes de *peoples* better here. One mastah we hab down de rice plantation was de wors'."

Then Auntie Dee whispered so Jack wouldn't hear. "Ebuh time mistress ain't lookin', he grabbin' at any young gal he can find. An' plenty beatin's come on us, too.

"Han's be wuk from fus' light in dem rice marsh. Come harvest time, go back out afta' supper an' work till get de crop cut an' tied in sheaves. Den has ta haul it all obuh de mill on flat boats. Onct sheaves is dere, gots ta t'resh an' winnow de chaff fuh millin'. An' de seed rice take muh wuk.

"All dat eben worse if y'all's racin' bad wedduh. Sometime hab work out un'er torch light. Plenty time work us till we couldn't move no muh—jus' sleepin' two, maybe t'ree hour a night."

"That's terrible."

"Yes suh. But tru all dat, I ain't nebuh had de whip, not onct."

"Really?"

"Nebuh. Sometime dey 'cuse me o' dis an' dat, keeps my food back or makes me work longer day. Dey jus' tryin' ta break me when I were young. Nebuh wuk d'ough. But was enough ta make Auntie Dee wunna learn how be de cook, ta git out dem snake-ridden rice marsh."

"Seems like it made you stronger," Aidan observed.

"Maybe da's right, Mr. Aidan. But dat bring me on ta sumpin' else. Mos' Gullahs has fait', some in de old way, but mos'ly in de new. An' dat fait' come outta' us in singin' an' makin' joyful noise ta de Lord wi' jus' 'bout anyt'ing we can lay a han' to—spoon, hoe, or jus' slappin' a knee."

"I like that," Aidan said. "Just use what you've got! God can't ask us for more."

"Da's right, Mr. Aidan. Say, you don't look like it on de outside, but maybe yuh has a li'l Gullah in yuh!" Auntie Dee teased. "But I tells yuh, de luckiest day o' my life come when dat ol' mastah down country go broke. Big storm come tru an' waste de whole crop. Whew! Money were tight ta begin wit'. But dat storm done him in. He took advertisement in de paper an' sold ebry las' one us slaves. Special auction man come out ta do de sale. We was all tol' git washt up! Look strong an' happy! Well, I jus' prayed, 'Lawd, gib me good mastah appreciate good wuk, an' Auntie wuk hard ta please, I promise.' When dey say some us comin' up Virginia Valley, our heart start ta soar. Slabes knows, much better livin' up here."

"I'm very glad you had the good fortune to come here, Auntie Dee."

"Me too, Mr. Aidan! OK, put li'l honey on yuh now, so's it feel good an' he'p yuh neck heal quick. Gwan put de bandage on loose so's ya gets some air unda dere. Da's it. Yuh neck fixt up good as I can fuh now. Look at it again, tumahruh.

"Thank you, Auntie Dee, for your excellent hospitality, and for dressing my wounds. Well, Jack, the bell will ring quarter past five before you know it. We'd better get some sleep."

"Ah, Pa, Mith Liza was just tellin' me about where to catch the biggest fish in the stream!"

"That reminds me," Aidan said, "what do we do about rations, or gettin' meals?"

Auntie Dee warmly offered, "Yuh fus' square meal be right here when yuh gets up tumahruh, Mr. Aidan. An' y'all welcome at Auntie's table any time. But we qwan fix ya up ta git what all hands gits fuh food. Den yuh can make some meals yuhself, jus' de way yuh likes 'em."

"Thank you for everything, Auntie Dee," Aidan said sincerely, as he extended a hand of friendship to her.

Auntie playfully brushed it aside and said, "Mistuh, yuh bes' come on in here fuh big ol' Auntie hug. We so glad yuh come all dis ways ta he'p us. God bless yuh!" she cooed as Aidan bent down and warmly embraced her.

Jack and Aidan floated back to their freshly scrubbed abode, and unfolded the clean bedding that Liza had provided.

Back in the kitchen, Liza and Auntie Dee chatted a bit more.

"Liza, where dat man's woman?"

"Oh, Auntie Dee, it's such a tragic story," Liza sighed.

"Wutchuh mean?"

"She was stricken ill on the voyage here from Ireland, and died along with the child inside her that was due any day."

"Lawd, no!" cried Auntie Dee. "Not de wife and momma ta dat dear man an' little boy. Tell me it ain't so!"

"It's true, Auntie Dee."

"Mm, mm, mmm."

The two women sat silently for a few moments, absorbed in their grief. Then Auntie said, "Dear Jesus, Mr. Aidan such a fine man. An' Liza, beliebe me, if dere one t'ing ol' Auntie good judge of, iz a *good man*!"

"I know, Auntie," Liza smiled.

"Gal, I lookt in dem blue-green eyes o' his an' it make Auntie Dee feel like a young gal again!"

"He loved his wife so dearly, Auntie. I'm sure it will be a good while before Aidan gives a thought to letting himself love again."

"Oh, I knows, Liza. An' don't go t'inkin' Auntie makin' like she young 'nuf ta git in line. Long pass' it. But I tells yuh dis. When he ready, some lucky gal gwan hit de jackpot!"

# Chapter 15

Bolstered by many prayers and the efforts of their new friends, Jack and Aidan made it through their first few days at High Meadows. Setting the forge right and straightening up their living quarters filled much of the time. Aidan also undertook his first real jobs. He replaced the outer rims of the wheels on a heavy wagon, and repaired springs on a two-wheeled cart.

When work finally wound down on Saturday afternoon, Aidan and Jack walked over to see Auntie Dee. Aidan asked, "Auntie, we were wonderin' if there will be a service for the Sabbath here tomorrow?"

"Well, Mr. Aidan, it ain't de fus' Sunday o' de mont'. So ol' reberan' dat come 'round den ain't due ta preach us."

"So what will you do?" Aidan asked.

"Oh," replied Auntie Dee, "we jus' has breakfas' an' strolls on down by de big oak. Den we sings our praises to de Lawd till we feels like we sung out. We talks a little, and sometime somebody pray. Da's chu'ch."

"Could Jack and I come join you?"

"Shuh can! We all like dat!"

The next morning after breakfast, Jack and Aidan joined Auntie Dee, Liza, about ten other adults and several children as they slowly walked down to the shade of a century oak. Aidan carried his Bible, and when everyone paused in the singing to catch their breath, Aidan asked if they would mind if he read from the scriptures. Several encouraged him, "Sho', please do!"

So Aidan read aloud from the third chapter of the book of John, culminating with verse sixteen, "For God so loved the world, that he gave his only begotten Son, that whosoever believeth in him should not perish, but have everlasting life."

The little congregation warmly thanked him for the reading. Emboldened by the way they had received the Word, Aidan asked, "Would you like to talk a bit about what we just heard?"

It was wonderful to see what happened next. Of course, Auntie Dee led the way.

"Well, Mr. Aidan, let Auntie Dee say fus' dat, eben d'ough yuh talks a li'l different frum all us on account o' where yuh comes frum, yuh reads da Word real nice. An' it good, too, dat yuh ain't preachin' *at* us wha' ta t'ink. 'Stead, yuh actually ast us what *we* t'inks. We likin' dat, too!"

Auntie Dee's sentiments were seconded all around.

Then Liza offered, "And the passage you chose is one of the most important in the whole Bible. It gives us God's promise that if we believe upon his son, Jesus, we will have eternal life."

This brought a cascade of comments.

"Shoot, dat just about de whole book, right dere!"

"Simple as a chile can understan' it."

"Amen!"

"Hallelujah! Amen!"

Aidan humbly accepted these comments, then asked, "Would anyone like to pray?"

"You pray, Mr. Aidan," shouted Essex. "You doin' good!"

And so he began, "Dear heavenly Father, we thank you for this chance to stop, be still, and worship you."

"Mm-hmm."

"And Father, we thank and praise you for this day, and the strength to live it. Help us ta live it in a way that will please and honor you. And we thank you for the blessin' of your mighty word. May it speak ta our hearts, our spirits, and to our minds. Let it strengthen and encourage us durin' the week ahead. We pray for any who could not join us today due ta sickness and other problems. Please grow and bless our fellowship, Lord. And we thank you for new friends who have allowed Jack and me ta worship here with them. In Jesus's precious name, amen."

Auntie Dee called out, "Mr. Aidan, you one humble white man!"

Aidan thoughtfully replied, "Auntie Dee, when I am with you all, I never think of any difference between us."

"Oh, you different, Mr. Aidan!" chimed in Julia, Auntie Dee's helper. "For one," she giggled, "we don't say you all. It's '*y'all!*'"

"I told you, Papa!" cried Jack.

"Boy right!" someone shouted, followed by general laughter.

Then they all got up, stretched, and began to slowly make their way back up to the slave quarter.

As they approached Auntie Dee's cabin, she startled everyone as she screamed loudly at an old man crouching beside the pathway.

"Lut'er! Git on out from here wit' yuh witchcraf'! Don't bodder dis here man. He a true man o' God. Git on outta here!" she yelled, waving her hands over her head as she chased him off.

"Auntie, what was that all about?" Aidan asked.

"Ah, ol' Lut'er, he frum de nex' place obuh. He say he were what I calls a witch doctah, back in Africa when he were young. He salt wadduh slabe—one dat come 'crost de sea.

He say he a healer. But everbody 'round here come ta Auntie Dee fuh *good* medicine, not ol' Lut'er's chicken bones an' incantation."

"Was he tryin' ta do somethin' ta me?"

"It jus' his nonsense. Dey calls it 'catch a shadow. He t'ink if he can catch a enemy shadow, den he hab powers obuh yuh."

"But why am I his enemy? I never hurt him."

"I knows, Mr. Aidan. But he hear you a Christian man dat read de Word. So in his mind, dat make you against his ol' ancestor ghosts an' demons. None o' us gib much stock anymuh ta what he belibe. Jus' ol' Lut'er do. But he say was a time when he hab big powers."

"What kind of powers?" Aidan asked.

"Well, witch doctah hab ta do sumpin' so's peoples keep comin' ta him. He mus' *show* his power. So, in Africa, he say he could walk de string. Dey stretches skinny little rope 'tween two tree, an' he say many time he walk on it, high up obuh ya head."

"I never heard of such a thing," Aidan marveled.

"An' he say sometime he let de village bury him alive. Den he jump out from behind 'em, an' scare 'em all ha'f ta death! Dat make lot o' peoples belibe in him."

"That sounds like he's in league with an evil spirit."

"Oh, he evil all right. But Lut'er say he mess up an' kill de daughter o' de village chief, cause he gib her bad medicine. Afta dat, chief gib Lut'er up ta slabe catchers, an' he wind up here. An' when he wind up here, he hab no mo'powers, jus' kind o' fakin' it is all."

"Do you think he would come to fellowship with us Sunday mornings?"

"Dat jus' like yuh, Mr. Aidan! Man like ta cast his bad juju on yuh, an' all yuh wants do is ast him come ta chu'ch. Yuh fuhgibs jus' like Jesus. Mm-hmm. Now I *knows* we got ourselfs a preechah!"

# Chapter 16

Jack and Aidan were at High Meadows a number of weeks before they met Mr. William Cauley when he visited the forge.

"Ah, the new smith! Glad you've joined us. William Cauley," the master said as he reached out his hand to Aidan.

"Aidan Smith. Pleased ta finally make your acquaintance, sir," Aidan said, as they shook hands warmly. "This is me son and me apprentice, Jack."

"And a good-looking lad he is. Hello, Jack."

"Hello, sir!" Jack replied, totally in awe of this tall, grand-looking man they had wondered so much about.

"Aidan, I want to extend my condolences about the loss of your wife."

"Thank you, Mr. Cauley."

"Was there any type of ceremony, or memorial made on her behalf?"

"No, sir. That has left kind of an empty spot in us, you might say."

"Well, then, we shall seek to fill it. Please write out your wife's full name, dates of birth and passing, and present them to Mrs. Cauley."

"Yes, sir. I'd be so grateful."

"We'll see what we can do. Now, Aidan, how are you finding your work here?"

"It's been steady, and familiar, sir."

"Good. You did a fine job on the heavy wagon and the cart. And I must apologize for the state of things as you found them. It was terrible what happened to old Dawson. He was a fine man in his day. But what do you need, now, to do your work properly?"

"Well, sir, I'd just been makin' do, best I could. But since ye ask, there are several things—iron stock for general use, and to make tongs and different-sized awls. And I hate ta mention such a costly thing, but the bellows is almost past mendin'."

"Yes, yes, I can see that, Aidan," Mr. Cauley said, as he inspected the deteriorated leather on the bellows. "Well, let's do this to make sure we don't miss anything. Ponder your needs for another day, and I'll be sure to check with you in the morning, before I leave for Mississippi."

"Mississippi, sir?"

"Of course, you wouldn't have heard. Our numbers are going to grow here at High Meadows. My uncle, Peter Simpson, passed from this life."

"I'm sorry, sir."

"Thank you. I have inherited six of his slaves. My man servant, Isaac, and I will start out tomorrow to retrieve them. I'll send an order for your supplies on to my commercial agent in Winchester before I go. Well, again, it is grand to have a working smith with us, and a willing helper to boot!"

"Thank you, sir. We shall endeavor to serve you well."

"Yes, sir. Me too, sir!" offered Jack.

"I'm sure you both will. Now, is there anything else you need before I go?"

Hesitantly, Aidan said, "Yes, sir." He went quickly to a shelf and retrieved a sealed envelope. "Is there a way I could send this letter to me family back home?"

Mr. Cauley smiled, took the letter and said, "I'll gladly see to it myself."

"Thank you, for everything, sir," Aidan responded.

As the master strode away toward the manse, Aidan's mind jumped back and forth between his highly favorable impressions of Mr. Cauley, and the news the master had conveyed. There was a chance their Sabbath fellowship was about to grow.

"He is a very nice man, Papa!"

"Yes, Jack. And there's a chance he's going to bring us some very nice, new friends!"

Mr. Cauley was gone until the weather began to turn cold. Their travel back from Mississippi was slow. Isaac drove with the new slaves aboard a wagon the master purchased from his uncle's estate. Except for a quick side trip to attend to state business in Richmond, Mr. Cauley accompanied the new slaves all the way home on his regal, black mount. He stayed with the wagon to protect the party, and to make provision for their food and shelter.

Auntie Dee was told about their journey soon after they arrived from Mississippi. A slave girl gave Auntie an account of the trip, and described her life down South.

"All right, chile, set yuh right down here by Auntie Dee's fire, an' drink a cup o' tea. I wants yuh tell me all about yuhse'f."

Shyly at first, the girl began, "My name is Chloe, Auntie Dee. I was born Chloe Bannister on plantation dey call Westfield, down Mississippi. Was about a day an' a half wagon ride out o' Hattiesburg."

"All right. Tell me all 'bout dat," Auntie Dee encouraged.

"When me an' my brother, Brister, was real little, we an' Momma got sold off ta bad mastah name Peter Simpson. His place up de road at Yellow Creek Plantation. I hate my life dere."

"Why's dat, chile?" Auntie Dee inquired.

"Ever since I was twelve or thirteen, I felt men's eyes on me. It taught me if I was gwan keep dey hands off me, I had ta learn ta kick, bite, and fight. But when dem eyes belongs to a white man, I found out dat fightin' jus' end up causin' mo' pain.

"I know," sympathized Auntie Dee. "Seen dat many a time."

"Brister were too young in de beginnin' to try'n stick up fo' me. An' Momma was too beat down. Weren't no fight lef' in her. But I keeps myself pure, till one day mastah make me move up de big house, work as a maid."

"Oh, Lawd," Auntie Dee said knowingly.

"Ever' time mistress go out, he come lookin' fo' me.

Chloe's face began to tremble, as tears welled in her eyes. "One night mistress go to special church meetin'. He come, caught me in a corner, an' . . . I couldn't get away! He weren't gentle wit' a young gal, Auntie. I still has nightmares 'bout it, him pawin' all over me and rippin' my clothes. When I couldn't stand it an' starts ta scream, he smash his forehead against my face ta shut me up. He broke my nose."

"No!" Auntie cried.

"Only good thing, Auntie, it knock me out. So I didn't have to know all what happen nex'. When I woke up, blood everwhares, and slave sistah, Julie, cryin' over me."

"Lawd, chile, yuh been t'ru it," Auntie Dee said as she reached out to console Chloe.

"He keep comin' to me ever time he get his chance. Aftah while, some time he give me dis an' dat to make look like he cares little bit. But seein' me wit' a pretty ribbon jus' make all dem other slave start callin' me 'missy.'"

"Dey wud!"

"I never know'd it meant I were his mistress. I jus' knew I didn't like it. Dat evil mastah make me hate men—all mens, but white mens in particular."

"Hab mercy," Auntie said.

"I figure out later, it was probly dat firs' time dat make me get wit' chile. By time I starts ta show, de mistress know'd I were his favorite. When she seen my belly swell, she try'n kick me right dere. He caught her at it, and say he'd *whip* her if she done it again.

"He say dat?"

"Uh huh. Dat were de only time he ever stuck up fo' me.

"When de baby come, she so pretty! Little button nose an' curly hair. When she close her eyes, eyelash look like painted on by God's own hand! Everbody say she look like a angel. So da's what I calls her, Angel."

"Da's God's blessin' on yuh," assured Auntie Dee.

"Um. But only one trouble. Her skin too white."

"Too white?" Auntie Dee asked.

"Say dat cause, when mistress seen her skin, it remind her who de daddy was an' she like ta go crazy! She throw'd me an' de baby out de house. So back down de slave quarter we goes. Aftah while, though, ol' mastah start missin' his comfort. So he tell me a nurse gwan come fo' de baby. He say, 'Don't worry, she'll take special good care of the child. You stay on here, but you'll see the baby real regular.'

"My mind jus' go 'round an' 'round, and I can't stop thinkin', *'Mastah, you can't take my baby!'* Den de nurse come one day by wagon. I say, 'I want's ta see her.'

"She look at me wit' sad ol' eyes like she were lookin' at someone 'bout ta lose all dat she had. Den she put de baby to her breas'. Baby start ta suck, den de driver smack reins on dem horses an' off dey goes!"

"Oh, Lawd!" cried Auntie Dee.

"I chase afta' dat wagon fo' all I's worth. Tears starts strea-min' down into my mouth while I screams, 'Stop! Stop!'

"Den I hears mastah shout out from behind me, 'Chloe!'

"I stops jus' long 'nuf ta turn an' shout at him, 'How could you?'

"By time I turns 'round, dat wagon long gone. I never forget dat day. I never forgets how de wet nurse look at me.

I never forgets how top o' my baby girl's head jerk when de wagon jump ahead cause driver whip dem reins. I never forget dat. And I never, ever seen my lil' baby girl again."

"Dear chile, come here and let Auntie hold ya," Auntie Dee said, and as she drew Chloe to her breast and rocked her.

"Auntie, I pray ta God I doesn't have wait till glory ta see my baby again."

"We pray you's gwan see her, chile," Auntie assured.

After a moment, Chloe continued, "Mistress's name were Helen Simpson. Turn out she an' mastah couldn't have no chilluns of dey own. Afta' what happen me, I know'd it was mistress dat were barren, not him."

"Mm-hmm. An'chile, jus' so it clear in yuh mind, yuh know dat yuh mistress down Mississip was de aunt ta *our* mastah here, Mastah Cauley."

"I knows. Still can't believe it, but I knows. An' guess was some justice come on her fo' what she done, cause about a year afta' my Angel was took away, mistress come down wit' pneumonia. Weren't no doctah close enough ta come, so slave sistah, Lucinda, (she come with us ta High Meadows), anyways, she come ta take care o' old mistress.

"Dat were hard on Lucinda, one, cause no one like de mistress. But hard, too, cause mistress modest 'bout her person. So Lucinda done tol' her, 'Mistress, ya has ta undress to de waist if I'm gwan tend to ya.'

"Den Lucinda make up a plaster, mos'ly from corn meal."

"Dat were right ta do," agreed Auntie Dee.

"Well, mistress didn't need ta be modest after all, cause when Lucinda get done wit' her, couldn't make out none o' her parts anyways from so much cornmeal she caked up in!"

Chloe snickered, and Auntie Dee laughed through lingering tears.

"Were hot corn meal, too, hot as mistress could stand it. Den Lucinda lay on cheese cloth wit' little lard rub on it, keep it from stickin'."

"Da's good too!"

"So da's how Lucinda keep mistress's chest warm, fo' days an' fo' nights. Fif' day, though, de sickness took her."

"Praise Jesus!"

"Mean as she were, Auntie, we feels *some* sorrow. An' slaves was worryin' 'bout what gwan happen next."

"Sure dey be."

"But didn't nothin' happen next. No new mistress, dat is. No need. De mastah have me. An' wit' no mistress ta hide from, he had me mos' any time he want.

"Ever time I pray, 'Dear Lawd, let dat be de las'.'

"Time go by, den I seen mastah don't come ta me fo' whole week. Den two. An' he start lookin' jaundice. Some say was too much liquor, an' eatin' cow meat ever day. Den he get worse an' worse, till he don't even go out de house."

"Da's bad."

"Mm. So one day ol' Lucas, he de butler, he tell us mastah dead. Den slaves *really* wonders what next!"

"Has to," Auntie Dee agreed.

"Finally Mastah Cauley come. Since he nephew to de mastah, he part inheritor all mastah own. So Mastah Cauley come ta get us.

"Auntie, I likes Mastah Cauley mos' right away, even though I hates his family, and I don't like white men. But somethin' in his eyes tell me he different. An' when he look at me, he look me in de eyes, not somewhares else."

"He right an' true!"

"We found out we was comin' here when ol' Lucas come to de quarter wi' piece paper seem real important. He say to us, 'Y'all listen up!' Den he start readin' lis' o' six slaves dat have my name on it. When he get done readin', he say, 'All dem what's been read, git you belongin's together. Y'all leavin' fo' Mastah Cauley plantation, way up de Virginia Valley. Y'all leavin' *tomorrow!*'

"So here dem slaves dat come north—James, de stable groom; my hot-temper brother, Brister; little Tim dat work in de dinin' room; Henderson—guess you say he a field hand, but so old, he mos'ly jus' stay in de quarter; Lucinda who do laundrin'; an' me, you know, Chloe.

"Five us rode up on de wagon while one walks. All could ride if need be, but mos'ly one or two gets off ta lighten de load and stretch dey legs. Mississippi up ta Virginny, da's a long ways. Bein' fall time, too, was lots o' rain. Mastah Cauley done good by us, though, findin' places we can sleep dry. Sometime we stoppin' at road house tavern where we stays in de livery. Sometimes stop at plantations he know. So he keep us dry, an' fed pretty good."

"Dat de kind o' man he is, Chloe," assured Auntie Dee.

"Well yesterday, we comes up de lane ta our new home! Mos'ly I remembers two things. One, seein' dat sign at end of de lane. Seen dem words, and don't know what dey says. But mastah say words is 'High Meadows.' An' we feelin' high, jus' lookin' at 'em!

"De second thing I remembers, after all dem dogs barkin', chillun comin' runnin', den you, Auntie Dee, Mr. Aidan an' his boy, maids lookin' out de big house windas, field hands strollin' up from de quarter; de second thing I remembers is de mos' beautifulest angel-face woman I ever seen, or ever will see. She come down de front steps an' take arm of de mastah. She Ms. Isabel. She come down dem porch step like she floatin' on a cloud. An' even in long skirt, she don't have ta watch where she steppin'!"

"I knows, chile!" laughed Auntie Dee.

"Firs' thing she say is, 'Welcome, all, to High Meadows, your new home.' Den she tell a boy he'p me down off de wagon. Ain't nobody ever think ta help me down off nothin' my whole life!

"Mastah say, 'Everyone, this is Chloe, Lucinda, Henderson, James, Brister, and Timothy. Let's welcome them!'

"I were dere, chile," reminded Auntie Dee.

"I knows. But it still surprise me, after mastah say welcome us, dat y'all did! Den mastah ast each one us say what we do. Which we done. Last thing, he ast y'all take us new *servants* to de quarter an' get us fed. We was all us still slaves, but felt mo' like we was jus' *peoples* fo' change."

"Chile, you still ain't tellin' Auntie Dee nothin' *new*!"

"I knows, Auntie. But I tellin' you, cause it were so new ta *me*!"

"I knows. Was same fuh me when I come up frum de lowlands."

"Well, whatever dey calls us, Auntie Dee, servant or slave, we all know'd one thing certain. Comin' up here ta Virginia Valley was a long, long ways from dem hot cotton fields down home!"

# Chapter 17

Jack and Aidan worked steadily to make their abode presentable.

One day, Jack asked Aidan, "Papa, does our place look good enough to start havin' our friends come visit like you said?"

Aidan looked around and realized that, though far from being a palace, their dwelling was probably about as good as it would get.

"I believe so, son. Who should we invite for a visit?"

"Miss Liza, *please*?"

"Oh, are you sure?" Aidan teased.

"Yes, Papa. Let's have her to supper!"

Aidan's Louisa had been a wonderful cook. She could make the most common cuts of meat taste like fare for a king. And her baking was even better. So Aidan never had cause, before, to learn his way around a kitchen.

Now, he and Jack were subsisting on a diet of porridge, potatoes, fresh fruit and some very well done beef. Those provisions were supplemented by a kindly supply of Auntie Dee's goodies.

"What do ye think we should prepare for our first guest ta eat?" Aidan asked.

"I already asked her what her favorite is."

"What?"

"She likes chicken in the oven, rice, and greens."

Laughing, Aidan said, "It sounds ta me like a whole plan's been hatched that I had nary a clue of."

"Oh, I was just wondering what she liked, Papa, that's all."

"Yes, and I'm the Prince of Wales. Well, we don't really have an oven, so it will have ta be chicken roasted on the spit. I know ya boil rice. And cookin'greens shouldn't be that much of a bother."

"And what about dessert, Papa?" Jack said, rubbing his tummy.

"I'll ask Auntie Dee if she wouldn't mind providin' us somethin', son."

As joyful an occasion as they hoped this first little dinner party would be, when they started to actually prepare for it, Aidan began to have his doubts. Jack was so unbelievably excited that he hardly slept for the two nights prior. And he drove Aidan half-crazy fussing about where each of them would sit, and where they could find napkins and a proper table cloth.

Aidan managed the preparations by asking himself, *"What would Louisa do?"*

Finally, the big event arrived when Liza did, carrying a beautiful bouquet to serve as their table's centerpiece.

"Oh my, gentlemen, how lovely your table looks with candles glowing! I hope you don't mind me bringing some flowers for us to enjoy."

Jack nearly burst with pride as he admired the setting for their repast. He described to Miss Liza their arduous preparations in what, Aidan thought, was an embarrassing amount of detail. But that only served to make their guest realize how much her presence meant to them.

Aidan's cooking seemed adequate, at least. Liza assured him that keeping rice from sticking together often takes years of practice. And the meal was capped with one of Auntie Dee's best "sweet 'tater" pies.

As Aidan cleared the table, Jack and Liza played at the cup and ball toy that Roebuck Chandler had given him. It was so nice, Aidan thought, *"ta have feminine joy and laughter in our humble home!"*

Later, after much cajoling, Jack prepared for bed. Then he came back in to say his prayers with the adults before shuffling (supposedly) off to sleep.

What a luxury it was, then, for Aidan to have Liza all to himself.

"Liza, you have been so kind to us, that I feel like I've known ye for years. But I really don't know anythin' of the details of your life. Could ye share a bit about it?"

"Oh, I'm not sure there's much of interest in my simple life. I grew up on the big place in the valley, one of eight children. Sickness took two brothers and a sister. All the rest of us worked hard, mostly too hard."

"I'm sorry for your losses," Aidan offered.

"Thank you. Only my father, Walter Moore, is still there. My mother passed away, not so long ago."

Seeing how the description of her difficult life was saddening him, Liza said, "Oh, I'm sorry, Aidan. I'm not good at telling stories, even my own. But my life is much better now. I have plenty to be thankful for!"

"Ta work for Mrs. Cauley, ye mean?"

"Yes, indeed. The mistress has been so very good to me. She's worked hard to educate me. She gives me access to her wonderful library. And I have to constantly ask her not to give me things that I might admire or show a fondness for."

"Why not?" Aidan asked, as he poured them more tea.

"I've learned that I need to remember my place here at High Meadows, and not appear to put on airs in front of the other servants."

"They would never think ill of you."

"Oh, you would be surprised! So, when I'm in the slave quarter, I just try to fit in."

"Fit in?"

"You know, in my speech and in my manner."

"But you must have worked very hard ta gain your knowledge."

"True. But I'm satisfied to be able to use proper grammar when I want to. I really don't prefer it over the way I talk with my friends."

"Liza, you are a very thoughtful woman."

"Why thank you, Aidan."

"Oh, I wanted to ask you about something, Liza. Today, when Essex and I went into Front Royal, we were stopped on the street by a man who asked to see a piece of paper Essex was carrying."

"His pass?"

"Yes, that's what he called it."

Liza explained, "He has to carry a pass any time he leaves the property. All slaves do. And the passes are for that specific date and purpose."

"I can't imagine havin' ta do that," Aidan proclaimed. "Who checks your pass?"

"Any white person can demand to see it. But at night, pattyrollers, or patrollers roam about, almost for sport. Sometimes they use dogs. They're often drunk. Snead's been known to go with them. I'd never be caught, alone, away from the property at night."

Aidan was highly irritated by this, and he asked, "How does all that make you feel?"

"If you let it, it'll make you feel less than human."

"Will I have to carry a pass?"

"No, Aidan. I did check with the mistress for you, to make sure. And she said that indentured servants don't have to."

"I'm sorry that you do, Liza. But . . . we were talkin' about happier things, like workin' for Mrs. Cauley. As I've seen first hand, you get to travel with the mistress."

"Oh, yes. That's the most exciting part of being Ms. Isabel's maid! We make shopping trips to Washington Town and Alexandria a couple times a year. I've also seen the family homes in Maryland, Staunton and Philadelphia."

"Ah, Philadelphia—Jack and I 'skipped through there' on our way ta High Meadows!" Aidan said with tongue in cheek.

"Oh dear;" cried Liza, recalling what Snead had done to Aidan. "Let me see how your neck is healing," she said, as she moved to Aidan's side to inspect his scars.

"With your help," Aidan whispered, "I'm just fine, Liza."

With their faces close together, they looked into each other's eyes for the briefest instant. Then Liza leaned back, smiled, and politely said, "Well, Mr. Smith, I want to thank you for a very lovely evening!"

Aidan sensed it was time to rise to say good-night, when Jack, who'd obviously been eaves dropping, appeared in the bedchamber doorway and called out, "Are you leaving, Mith Liza? Did you like our party?"

Liza bounded over to Jack and gave him a kiss and warm embrace.

"How could I not!" Liza exclaimed.

Aidan was almost feeling left out until she said, "Jack *and* Aidan, I loved every minute of it!"

# Chapter 18

"Good mo'nin', Liza!"

"Auntie Dee, what brings you over to the manse this morning?" Liza asked, as she worked with the mistress's wardrobe.

"Oh," replied Auntie coyly, "jus' brought some dem fancy scones, fresh out de oven fuh mistress. Has some lef' over, jus' in case yuh wants stop by."

"Woman, you know I can't resist," replied Liza, as she quickly hung up a pair of Mrs. Cauley's robes. "I'll ask Ms. Isabel and be right over!"

As Liza entered Auntie's kitchen, Auntie Dee said, "Dere yuh is, gal. Yuh wants some tea?"

"What's a scone without tea?"

"Jus' bein' polite! Dere, now, let's hab a nice sit down," Auntie Dee said, as she proudly presented Liza a plate of fresh scones, butter, raspberry jam, and a cup of sugary tea.

Mm!" proclaimed her guest, "You've outdone yourself, Auntie."

"Well, jus' tryin' keep up wit' dat *man* been cookin' fuh yuh! By de way, how dinner go las' night?"

"It was charming."

"Charmin'? What yuh mean?"

"I mean that my two male hosts went above and beyond makin' me feel special."

"Oh, now yuh talkin'! Wha' dey surb?"

"What I asked for," replied Liza matter-of-factly. "A beautiful roast chicken, rice, and greens. And your sweet potato pie was excellent. These scones ain't bad, either."

"Good. So, what y'all talk about?" asked Auntie excitedly, as she brushed some crumbs from her bosom.

"First, Jack talked about how they fussed and fussed gettin' ready for me to come till, I swear, his papa's face turned bright pink!"

"Wisht I could o' seen dat!" laughed Auntie.

"And they just welcomed me, and thanked me for being good to them. It was really very nice."

"Nice. Um hmm. An' did yuh and Mr. Aidan get ta spend some time *alone*?"

"Oh, just a few minutes after Jack turned in. He really didn't want to go to bed, but his papa won out in the end."

"I *bet* he did!"

"Now what's *that* supposed to mean?" Liza asked defensively.

"I means Mr. Aidan a good lookin', healt'y man. Why wouldn't he want ta be alone wit' a pretty young gal like yuh?"

"Auntie, we've been all through this. The poor man's wife hasn't been gone long enough for him to be half over it. You shouldn't say such a thing!" Liza protested.

"All Auntie Dee sayin', chile, is one day Mr. Aidan gwan be all de way obuh dat hurt. Den nature shuh 'nuff take its course."

"Fine," agreed Liza. "I'm sure there is a very nice white woman of the working class that'll make a fine mate for Mr. Aidan."

"Humph!" replied Auntie Dee.

# Chapter 19

Jack and Aidan made it through the rest of their first year at High Meadows well enough. But Aidan dreaded Christmas's approach as Louisa had always done so many things to make the season special.

In the midst of his growing gloom, Aidan had all but forgotten about Mr. Cauley insisting that he give the mistress the correct spelling of Louisa's name, and the dates of her birth and passing. But on Christmas Eve, the Cauleys hosted a grand party on the front porch of the manse with food, singing, a warming fire on the lawn and gift giving.

Mr. Cauley said, "Aidan, I have a little something for you. It has a bit of weight to it." Then he carefully handed Aidan a beautifully wrapped object about the size of a loaf of bread. The master quickly beckoned to Mrs. Cauley, and she joined them.

Aidan was surprised that the package felt as hard as a rock. It was, in fact, the most beautiful, small headstone with "Louisa Anne Smith" cut boldly into the top surface. It listed the dates of her life. Then on the front face, which was set on an angle to be visible from above, Aidan and Jack read the flowing inscription, *"Dearly Loved By Husband and Son"*

"It is granite, Aidan," the master explained. "It will last for the ages, and not crumble like the limestone hereabouts."

"Thank you, sir! And thank you, Mrs. Cauley," Aidan said in astonishment.

He thought it must be the finest stone engraving he'd ever seen. Jack was amazed as well, and they continued to thank the master and mistress profusely. They believed that Louisa was united with the Lord Jesus in heaven. But having this permanent way to memorialize her meant the world to them.

They kept the headstone on a sturdy shelf in the forge until a fine day the following spring, when a dedication service was held in the slave graveyard.

The Cauleys joined the slaves gathered there, as Jack and Aidan shared a few light and joyful things about Louisa with their friends. Aidan read aloud a Bible passage of God's assurance that all will live forever, with him, if they accept his Son as Messiah. Then they placed the headstone on a space Aidan had cleared and boxed in with a clever iron base to secure the stone. The spot was intentionally chosen near a corner of the graveyard where flowers were in bloom. Louisa had always raised and kept beautiful flowers in and around their home.

All of these events helped Jack and Aidan lay Louisa properly to rest. The way they were able to speak of her that day—calmly, and with the fondest memories, proved to Aidan that their hearts were beginning to mend. And all those assembled felt blessed to learn about Louisa.

Some weeks after the memorial, a fierce rain storm popped up without any warning. Jack was playing in the yard of the manse with Jonathan Cauley, while Aidan went out to the upper meadow mending fences. Aidan was unaware that Liza had gone into the meadow opposite to pick a basket of wild flowers.

There was an old drying shed between the pastures that hadn't been used since the master's grandfather grew tobacco. Suddenly, a thunderclap shook the earth beneath Aidan and he ran for the shed! He was startled to see Liza running in from the opposite direction.

They called wildly to each other, "Hurry!" as their nervous laughter mixed with dread of the ominous, dark clouds racing in overhead.

Then, in their last few strides before reaching the shelter, the blackened sky burst! In an instant, they were both drenched to the bone. As they entered the shed, Aidan offered Liza his vest to restore her modesty. She'd just wrapped it nearly twice around herself when suddenly, the roof above them flashed white-hot with a deafening ka-boom!

The lightning blast launched Liza several feet off the ground, only to land in Aidan's lap as he tumbled to the floor. He cradled Liza in his arms as she nearly squeezed the life out of him.

"Dear God, Aidan!" she cried, "We're gonna die!"

Though the lightning had definitely unsettled him, Aidan spoke softly, as he gently stroked Liza's hair.

"We're all right now, lass. It ne'er strikes the same place twice."

It felt so good to Aidan to comfort a woman again. In a few moments, Liza's fear began to subside.

As the storm passed on, Liza became uneasy with them continuing to hold each other, so Aidan regretfully obliged her. As they disentangled and stood to look out at the quieting conditions, Aidan could sense an obstacle that Liza was placing between them.

It made him sadly wonder if he would ever feel the warmth of her strong embrace again.

# Chapter 20

After the storm, Liza and Aidan walked back from the meadow to Auntie Dee's kitchen in silence. Liza's face showed a mix of embarrassment at what had happened in the drying shed, and some other emotion. Aidan still wasn't sure what it was. But he sensed it would be foolish, now, to push her to explain.

When they reached the kitchen, Aidan retrieved Jack who, along with Jonathan, had also been caught in the downpour. Auntie had both of them nearly dry by the fire and full of cookies, of course.

Because of the uneasiness he felt, Aidan excused Jack and himself by saying he wanted to, "go dry off at the forge." Liza stayed on to warm herself at Auntie Dee's fire.

"Mister Aidan run off kinda sudden, Liza. Sumpin' happen 'tween y'all out dere? An' why was ya wearin' de man's ves' when yuh come back in from de field?"

"I don't think I want to talk about it."

"Den yuh come to de wrong place, gal. Come on now. Dis Auntie Dee's kitchen yuh sittin' in!"

"Oh, Auntie, I acted such a fool."

"Wuhchuh mean?"

"I mean it was like I threw myself on him. But I didn't mean to, I swear."

"*Throw'd* yuhself on him? Come on, now. Tell me all 'bout dat!" Auntie Dee said, with great anticipation.

"The *lightning,* Auntie, it was the loudest noise I ever heard. I swear, it blew me up in the air and I just landed right in Aidan's arms."

"Dear, dear chile, when yuh gwan stop denyin' yuh feelin's fuh de man? I done *tol'* yuh, way back, he de man fuh *yuh*!"

"And I know better," Liza said. "We're too different to belong together. Even a child could see that!"

"What? Jus' cause yuh skin different? Somebody onct tol' me Irishmens is jus' like us, only God turned dem inside out!"

"Shush, Auntie. I don't want to laugh now," Liza said, trying not to snicker.

"All right, don't laugh. But leas'wise try usin' yuh head! Yuh *knows* yuh cares 'bout Mr. Aidan, an' little Jack too. On top o' dat, de dear little boy really do love yuh."

"Oh, Auntie, stop! You're just making it worse."

"Good! I wants ta make it so worse, yuh finally comes ta yuh senses."

"I have enough sense to realize the price we'd all pay for me marrying a white man."

"Now jus' a minute, an' hold on! Yuh really gwan try tell me yuh scared 'bout what other people says, even if it keep yuh from bein' happy? Shoot, gal, I thought yuh has muh sense an' backbone den dat! De only one else yuh oughts eben t'ink 'bout what dey says is mistress. An' I *knows* what she say. She say, 'Does yuh love him? Good, den do it!'"

"You know something, Auntie? It's almost *because* of Ms. Isabel that I feel this way."

"What in de world yuh talkin' 'bout now? Dat woman done all she could fuh yuh."

"I'm not saying I'm not grateful that she's helped me learn to read and dress up and go travel. But she's also shown me what it *really* means to be a lady. Believe me, I've watched her—the way she thinks, the way she handles herself, and how she takes everything in stride, even with her husband four days' ride away."

"I knows dat. So what *is* yuh sayin'?"

"I'm saying that, after seeing all she does, I don't care how many books I read or taffeta dresses I put on. I'll never be like Ms. Isabel."

"Gal, hush! Don't yuh ebuh dare talks like dat again! Yuh has de bes' chance *any* us gots, ta rise up an' be mo' dan jus' a slabe. Yuh gettin' all dat book learnin' an' dat is de *key*. Don't yuh sell dat short! It gwan make yuh *free* someday. Yuh has ta *beliebe* dat, so's de res' o' young folk 'round here knows dey can do it *too*! Dis ain't jus' 'bout Miss Liza, now. Dis 'bout *all* o' us."

Liza hugged Auntie Dee, and they both cried.

"Dere, dere. I knows it ain't easy, chile," Auntie comforted Liza. "Bein' first at anyt'ing ain't easy. Lawd, how I knows. But God'll he'p. Jus' keep prayin' an' countin' on him."

"But Auntie Dee, my mind is so mixed up about Aidan. I know he isn't like other men. I know he's full of God's spirit. And I admit, I don't know if it's just that I'm afraid his first wife would always be there between us. But I do know that I'm afraid to let my feelings go. And sometimes, I even wonder what God thinks about black and white together."

"My, my, my," Auntie Dee lamented.

"I love you, Auntie Dee," Liza said, as she dejectedly picked up her basket of flowers and turned to walk slowly back toward the big house.

Suddenly, Auntie Dee rushed to the kitchen doorway and yelled out after Liza, "Gal, befuh yuh go makin'up yuh mind what *God* t'ink about it, how 'bout dis? Who yuh t'ink it was done *made* dat big lightnin'?"

# Chapter 21

As far as anyone at High Meadows could see, Phineas Snead only had one friend in the Virginia Valley. In fact, "friend" may have been too strong a word. He had only one friendly acquaintance, a man named Jake Stellar, the local gunsmith.

"Morning, Mr. Snead. What brings you forth this fine day?"

"Morning, Stellar. Day seems like any other to me. Need lead and powder, per usual."

"Fine, but have to tell ya, price o' lead went up two cents."

"Like everything else. Can't you hold that down for a regular customer?"

"Not if I want to stay in business, Mr. Snead. Just put on fresh coffee, though. Will you take a cup?"

"Might as well get somethin' for my two cents. Take it black."

"Best way. Here you are," said Jake, handing him a cup as he motioned for Snead to take a seat. To make conversation he asked, "Snead, it occurs to me, I've never really asked you where you hail from originally."

Snead hesitated, then said, "Long as what I say stays in this room. Never liked too many people knowin' my business."

"On my word," Jake pledged, with an upraised hand.

"Well," Snead began reluctantly, "I was born and raised down on the James River. Father was a boatman, so he was mostly gone. Mother was a cook. Now they're both gone."

"Sorry to hear it."

"No matter."

After a pause, the strong coffee seemed to start to loosen Snead's tongue a bit. "I apprenticed to a cooper on the plantation when I was young. But I didn't take to it, or the cooper for that matter. I like workin' with my hands, all right. But a wooden barrel is a wooden barrel. Once you've made a few, your mind tends to wander."

"Um, like usin' a plane on a pile of gun stocks."

"So," continued Snead, ignoring Jake's comment, "prospects there didn't seem like much—years o' savin' every penny to buy my own tools. Then it'd be years more till I could buy out the old cooper."

"So what did you do?"

"One day the plantation boss was shorthanded," Snead said with a sense of pride. "It was harvest time, and he couldn't be everywhares. In them days in Richmond, a white boy had more standin' than any full-grown niggah. So the foreman had me oversee twenty pickers in a field. And, by God, I kept them to task!"

Chuckling, Jake Steller said, "I bet you did!"

"Got a little bit older, and I learned to use a whip like no one's ever seen. I could take the hat off a slackin' niggah quicker'n lightning. And when it come to doin' real punishment, I learned to make them never want it again."

"I see," said Jake quietly.

"Not that I've used a whip much up here," bemoaned Snead. "Darkies know not to push me to it, though. And I learnt another skill back home," he said, with the trace of a smile. "What ta do with that lead you overcharge for!"

"You've showed me that out back on many a tin can."

"Well," continued Snead with a rare, magnanimous comment, "I admit I'm grateful to Master Cauley for the Colt pistols I carry. Fine, fine side arms."

Jake agreed, "Everyone hereabouts says Cauleys is good folk to work for and deal with."

"We get along, Stellar. Cauley knows I'll drive his slaves, get a crop planted, raised, and sold to market. That and I keep the place safe when he's away, including his wife."

"That's a woman worth protectin'."

"If you say so. Anyhow, I eat well, have clothes on my back, a good horse and saddle."

"Sounds like you're a man who's got all he needs," observed Stellar.

"All but one thing. Nights get pretty cold and lonely up in this valley. 'Tween you and me, Stellar, I could use a little something to keep me warm—somethin' good to look at."

# Chapter 22

Essex had never married, but he was starting to think about it. Most of his marrying thoughts turned toward Julia, Auntie Dee's helper. That made him manufacture reasons for showing up at Auntie's kitchen.

"Hello, young lady!" Essex said, as he found Julia smoking her pipe on the kitchen's back door stoop.

"Essex, what you doin' 'round here middle o' de mo'nin'?" Julia asked playfully.

"Oh, jus' come by ta see if Auntie Dee have somethin' keep my stomach from growlin'."

"I heard dat, Essex!" Auntie Dee called out in mock anger from the doorway. "Here, dese two biscuits, an' a cup o' water gwan hab do yuh. By de way, where Snead?"

"He off buyin' gunpowder," Essex replied. Taking the warm biscuits and water, he said, "I'm grateful, Auntie Dee," and gave her a wink.

"Don't go winkin' on me, yuh ol' tomcat! I knows who yuh really comes 'round here lookin' fuh. Julia habin' her smoke break. But gal, when yuh gets done puffin' one bowl on dat pipe, git yuhself back in here."

"Yes, Auntie," Julia sighed.

"Gal how you doin'?" Essex asked Julia.

"Tolerable, Essex, tolerable. You?"

"Feelin' pretty good lately."

"Why's dat?" Julia wondered.

"Oh, jus' has a song on my heart mos' o' de time."

"Cause you an' Mr. Aidan makin' dat Sunday music?"

"Music fo' every day o' de week! By de way, when we gwan make a song fo' you?"

"I ain't got nothin' ta sing about."

"Gal, don't blaspheme! You has ta count your blessin's."

"I know," Julia said, as she moved away from the doorway to sit down on a log bench with Essex, "But some days, (whispering) I gets tired fetchin' all de time. I's a pretty good cook myself, Essex. Wisht I could step out an' be a cook on my own somewheres."

"Wisht I was *free!*" Essex said, as he started on his second biscuit. "But in de meantime, I know de Lawd watchin' over me."

"Well, still don't know 'bout makin' no song."

"Mr. Aidan a good listener, Julia."

"I likes Mr. Aidan," Julia said thoughtfully. "I really do. Course, firs' off, didn't really know what ta make o' him, him bein' de firs' fresh Irishman I seen."

"What you mean 'fresh'?" Essex wondered.

"You know, one dat jus' come here, an' still talkin' all funny like dat. Plus, was dat business o' him killin' a man."

"I know. Had some dem thoughts, too," Essex admitted. "But didn't take long fo' I seen he were a man full o' Jesus. He smart, too, but humble. An' he strong! Stonger'n bes' field hands we got."

"Oh yeah, I seen dem Irish muscles!"

"Dat pipe out yet?" Auntie Dee interrupted.

"Jus' about, Auntie Dee," replied Julia.

Essex stood up from his perch. "Thanks fo' de biscuits, Auntie Dee."

"You welcome, Essex," Auntie said, as Essex handed her the cup. "Bes' get on fuh Snead git back."

Julia knocked the smoldering ash from her pipe and called after Essex, "I'll try, Essex."

"Try what, gal?"

"Try'n make a song."

"Praise God Almighty!" Essex cried out, as he added a little skip to his step.

# Chapter 23

Auntie Dee, of course, was respected by all of the High Meadows slaves. It's true that she demanded as much. But most were genuinely fond of her. There was one fellow slave, though, that she had a special friendship with—Fanny, the laundress.

One memorable morning on a visit to the kitchen, Fanny shouted out, "Hey, Auntie Dee!"

"Fanny! Ain't dey keepin' yuh busy obuh yonder?"

"Oh, thought I'd come by, tell ya gwan need some laundry soap."

"Lawd, Fanny, ain't got time ta make a batch now. How long can yuh las'?"

"Two days I 'spose."

"Da's fine. I get to it. But dis time yuh has ta finally do it *wit'* me, so's yuh can learn. Any good laundress need ta make her own soap. An' now yuh hab new helper from down South. Yuh needs make dat soap ta show, Fanny de *head* laundress!"

"But Auntie, I can't make it like you. Remember when my hands was gettin' all dry an' crackin'?"

"Mm-hmm. Put goat milk in de mix. Make it sof' an' smooth. But yuh can learn, Fanny. Auntie teach yuh. Now, where Snead?"

"He watchin' 'em down bottom field."

"All right. Yuh wants some tea?"

"Mm-hmm. Jus' regular kind."

"Now listen dat! Yuh t'ink I'm gwan bring out sumpin' special fuh yuh, an' ain't eben holiday or yuh bir'day needer? Shoot, dis here gettin' like some buckruh tea room," Auntie Dee said, to heckle her friend.

"Jus' sayin', Auntie, regular mo' dan good enough fo' me!"

"Mm, mm, mm. Well, here yuh is. Now, Fanny, sit down an' tell me how dat *man* been treatin' yuh?"

"Zeb? He bes' treat me good, or I let somebody else bark up dis tree."

"Hah! Listen yuh, actin' like ebry man in de county gettin' in line, jus' ta say ullo. Yuh already has a good man, Fanny."

"I knows. But he think I'm doin' him a favor, so dat keep him interested."

"Da's right. Jus' remember, dey don't come 'round like him muh dan onct."

"I knows. Even wif' him workin' down de valley, I hears 'bout all he doin'. He can make ya rope bed, shelfs, kitchen cupboard, or build a whole spring house. Man handy 'bout all he do."

"Da's good!"

"Mm-hmm. An' he respect me, too. I know he want us lie down together, but I tol' him, I's much a lady as a laundress can be. So you know what he say?"

"Wha's dat?" Auntie asked as she leaned forward a bit.

"He askin' his master *buy* me so's we live de same place. Den we marry."

"Lawd God Almighty!" Auntie shouted with glee.

"Yeah, Auntie Dee, I thought on it every which way an' prayed on it, too. I figures if Zeb can convince dat ol' Dutchman spend dat kinda money, leas' I can do say yes."

"Lawd, Lawd, Fanny!" Auntie Dee said as she jumped up to hug her friend. "What a day dat will be! Gwan miss you, gal!"

"I knows, Auntie Dee. Miss you, too. Me an' you been here de longest."

"Mm-hmm. Fanny, I remembers what yuh was like when yuh firs' come here," Auntie Dee said, as they both re-took their seats.

"What ya mean, Auntie?"

"Yuh all de time runnin' obuh here tellin' me some amazin' t'ing 'bout Ms. Isabel."

"Like what?"

"Oh, like how her waist were so tiny, an' how ebryone try gettin' her ta eat muh, but she still only eat one biscuit."

"She still eat like dat!"

"Mm-hmm. Den yuh come waltzin' in here, pretend like yuh her. Put feather or piece ribbon in yuh hair, start sashayin' round like a lady."

"I done dat?"

"Course yuh done dat, many a time!"

"Jus' never seen nobody like her, Auntie Dee."

"I knows. Well, yuh jus' make shuh, in yuh man's eyes, he nebuh see nobody like Fanny!"

"Gwan try, Auntie Dee. You know I'm sho' gwan try!"

# Chapter 24

After worship, one Sabbath, Aidan was to sit with Fanny and Auntie Dee for a bit to see if Fanny's good news about getting married had given her the makings of a song.

Liza volunteered to keep Jack busy. She arranged for them to have a little tea party on the side porch of the manse.

"This is real nice, Miss Liza," Jack said. "I never saw a teapot like that pretty one with birds on it before."

"The mistress said we could use it. She is very fond of you, Jack. And," Liza said, uncovering a plate of tea sandwiches with a little flair, "I've made us some lunch!"

Jack's eyes seemed to get as big as their teacups. Liza managed to get his attention just long enough to say grace before he dug in.

Liza enjoyed this special time for just the two of them, as their sweet relationship was beginning to grow. When their meal was winding down, Liza softly said, "Jack, would you mind if I asked you a question?"

"I wouldn't mind, Miss Liza."

"Could you tell me a little about your mother?"

"I miss her."

"I'm sure you do, Jack. And if it's too hard to speak of her, we don't have to."

"No, I can do it. I'm getting used to it now. And Papa told me it doesn't mean I don't still love her."

Liza said, "Your Papa is very wise," as her eyes started to glisten.

"Well," continued Jack, "she was pretty. And she wasn't fat or anything."

"Oh, I'm sure not."

"No, but she was still soft. Her hands were real soft, and warm."

"Mm."

"She would always brush my hair with one hand and hold my cheek in the other hand. I liked that."

"Sounds wonderful!"

"And she always smelled good. Sometimes she would put something in her hair that smelled good. Then she would smell like that."

"And, what did she look like, Jack?"

"Well, sometimes people say I look like her."

"Really? That's nice to know," Liza said, as she studied Jack's face with new interest.

"Yeah, and I don't mind. I mean, a boy doesn't want to look like a girl."

"No, of course not."

"But I think it's OK if you still look like a boy, but parts of you look a little like someone else, if they're nice. So, she sort of looked like me but she had longer hair. It was still curly though."

"She sounds beautiful. Was she a happy person?"

"You could always tell when she was happy, because she would sing. Papa mostly just whistles, unless it's church time. But Momma, she would sing the real words while Papa whistled."

"That sounds nice."

"She loved Jesus. She loved Papa and me a lot, too. But I think she loved Jesus most of all."

"I can see why you miss her so much. But do you know what?"

"What?"

"I think that you and your papa are still lucky to have such good memories of your wonderful momma. And as you go on and live your life, you will make up your mind and decide what to do many, many times because of what you know your momma would say."

Jack thought about that for a moment. "I do that sometimes because of Momma, and sometimes because of Papa. It just depends."

"Yes. And that is why you have been so lucky to have such a good momma *and* papa. That will never ever go away, Jack."

Jack got up from his chair and hugged Liza.

"I'm glad you are nice to me, and Auntie Dee, too."

"Thank you, Jack," Liza said, as she embraced him warmly. "I like having you as my friend, too. And I bet your momma would have liked Auntie Dee!"

"I know she would. Auntie seemed like she liked me even before we got here. She was ready to be nice to me right away. And she's the best cook, ever, in the whole world."

"She always remembers to make you cookies!"

"Um hmm."

As Jack's gaze returned to the last tea sandwich on the plate, a look of doubt crossed his face as he pondered whether he could finish one more.

Then he said sincerely, "And you make a very nice lunch, Miss Liza."

# Chapter 25

Even with the success and joy of the Sunday worship services, there were some of the High Meadows slaves who did not attend. But those who did, prayed for all the others. And they tried to be alert to any chance to encourage everyone to come.

Jupiter, the High Meadows woodcutter, visited Aidan on his rounds several times a week. "Mornin', Mr. Aidan," he said, as he wheeled a handcart full of firewood into the forge.

"Jupiter, Good Mornin'. You're early today."

"Had extra wood lef' over cause mastah gone an' de mistress retire early. So I got round ta loadin' what you needs a li'l sooner today."

"Nice to get a break like that, isn't it?"

"It's a gif'. Da's how I sees it."

"The mistress is a strong woman to manage this place on her own so much of the time," Aidan observed.

"Shoot, dang right! An' tell you what, she nice, an' all. But she don't miss nothin'!"

"I've noticed that," Aidan chuckled.

"Right, an' tell ya sumthin' else, Mr. Aidan. She know her wood!"

"Really?"

"Want dis kind wood fo' here, dat fo' dere. Like, if big company comin', she like apple wood in de front parlor. Make it smell good. But in de dinin' room, she want beech cause it make a fire dance an' de room look all pretty."

"And you always bring me ash."

"Yes suh! Straight grain split easy, and give forge de mos' heat, jus' de way you likes it."

"There are tricks to every trade, aren't there, Jupiter?"

"Well, been doin' dis since I were thirteen year old."

"You cut for the whole place when you were that young?"

"Actually, was a old man, Louis, cuttin' when I started. He taught me rule number one."

"What's that?"

"Keep a sharp ax," Jupiter said with authority.

"That's smart. What's rule number two?" Aidan asked.

"Let de *ax* do de work."

"Just like my hammer," Aidan agreed.

"Same thing. But it take skill, don't it?"

"Wore myself out quick till I learned," Aidan admitted.

"See! Ya gots ta learn stay loose, so's ya *whips* de ax. It almos' like you castin' out a fishin' pole."

Aidan mimicked that motion.

"Da's it. Kain't try ta muscle it. No suh!" proclaimed Jupiter.

"It's still work, though," Aidan contended.

"Oh my, yes. But I learned singin' make de work go a little bettah."

"We sing a good bit at service, Sunday mornings. Why don't you join us this week, Jupiter? We'd love to have you."

"Don't mean no disrespect, Mr. Aidan. But I don't care ta come."

"Well let me ask then, why not?"

"I heard you helpin' slave sing 'bout der lives."

"Yes. We all seem ta have a story to tell, don't you think?"

"Oh, got me a story. Dat ain't de question."

"What is then, Jupiter?"

"It's what's *in* dat story. Cause, ya see, Mr. Aidan," he said sheepishly, "jus' 'tween you an' me, I gots women troubles."

"Any man with blood in his veins runs into some kind o' troubles," Aidan observed. "What's yours?"

"Ain't never been able ta git married. But dat don't stop me takin' liberties wi' certain gals. None 'round here on dis place, mind. But I ain't never been one o' dem hypocrites dat sin Saturday night, den start prayin' Sunday mo'nin'. Jus' kain't seem ta stop, is all."

"I have good news for you."

"What you mean, Mr. Aidan?"

"Admittin' that you have a problem and that you can't fix it yourself, is exactly what God wants to hear. Do you think he is big enough to help fix your problem?"

Essex reflected for a moment, then said, "If he have a mind to."

"He definitely has a mind to. Let's pray and ask him."

Pray they did. Eventually, Jupiter helped pen a song that got him back on track when he strayed. And the song helped keep a strong, steady beat for his ax. Jupiter also started to seriously contemplate marriage for the first time.

## Hep Me Not Ta Stray (Slow Tempo)

Oh-oh it's mo'nin' an' I'm sayin'
What I said so many time,
Lawd, why'd I have ta do dat
Take dis darkness offa' my mind.

Mm-hmm is easy when I get up
To say, "I be yours today,"
But den da nighttime start pullin' on me
Till you seem so far away.

CHORUS

Ohhhh he'p me stan' beside you, Jesus
He'p me not ta stray,
Pull me on up closer while
You push my sins away.
Dey kain't stay where you are
Dey don't like de bright o' day,
Ohhhh he'p me stan' beside you, Jesus
Please he'p me not ta stray.

I know, Lawd, you want me
Ta be mo' like you today,
By learnin' from you word
An' by doin' what it say.

Now dat I thinks about it
I know how I'm gwan ta pray,
Dat your light shine so bright on me
All my sins git up an' get out de way!

CHORUS

Ohhhh hep me stan' beside you, Jesus
Hep me not ta stray,
Pull me on up closer while
You push my sins away.
Dey kain't stay where you are
Dey don't like de bright o' day,
Ohhhh hep me stan' beside you, Jesus
Please hep me not ta stray.
Hep me stand beside you, make me
Mo', make me mo' like you today!

# Chapter 26

One morning in Mrs. Cauley's presence, Liza was straightening the things on the mistress's dressing table when she dropped an expensive bottle of imported perfume.

"Oh, Mistress, I'm so sorry!" Liza cried, as she placed the cut glass stopper back atop the elegant bottle.

"Don't worry, Liza. Only a drop or two spilled. And now it will smell of lilies in my bedchamber this morning."

"Oh, thank you, Mistress," Liza said gratefully, as she tried to catch her breath.

"But Liza, are you feeling yourself today?" Mrs. Cauley asked.

"Yes, Mistress. I'm—"

"I think I know you well enough to sense that something is troubling you."

Somewhat embarrassed, Liza admitted, "It would be hopeless to try and hide anything from you, Mistress."

Seated on the edge of her bed, Mrs. Cauley said, "Come, sit for a moment," as she patted the exquisite bed covering beside her.

"Oh, mistress, I couldn't!"

"I'm telling you that I want you to. Now, what is the matter?"

Liza thought before speaking, as she eased herself onto the very edge of the Cauley's bed. "Mistress, how do you always know what to do?"

"What do you mean, Liza?"

"I mean, you always seem so certain about things. You always say the right thing, and do the right thing."

"Oh, my!" replied the mistress, holding a hand to her bosom. "How I wish that were always true!"

"It is, ma'am. You just have this perfect way of knowing what's right and doing it. I hardly ever feel that way."

"Liza, why do you think I chose you as my trusted helper? It's because I really do have faith in you. In large part, that's because I value your own good judgment."

"Thank you, Mistress. But I don't always feel sure about my thoughts, or in deciding what to do. And I can't imagine that I ever will."

"Well," said Mrs. Cauley, "truth is, I didn't feel very confident when I was young either."

"I can't believe that, Mistress."

"It's true, Liza. And believe me, I certainly wasn't prepared to become the wife of an important man like Mr. Cauley."

"How do you mean, ma'am?" asked Liza.

"Oh, I had a decent background, all right. But I had a very different life before all of this." Mrs. Cauley said, waving a hand about in reference to the grandeur of High Meadows.

"Please tell me what your life was like, ma'am."

"Well, all right. I grew up on Maryland's Eastern Shore where Father became what they refer to as a 'self-made man.' His father was killed in an accident at sea. And his mother, Juniper—"

"Juniper, Mistress?"

"I know. It's so old-fashioned," said Mrs. Cauley with a chuckle. At any rate, poor grandmother, it is said, died soon thereafter of her grief."

"That's so sad, Mistress."

"Yes, and that was when my father was just a boy of ten. But little Henry Lewis Sargeant soon set about working at errands for an export merchant named Joseph L. Picard, in the port of Annapolis. He took Father on as his apprentice. In the process, Papa learned the commercial trade. In his teen years, he was actually entrusted with running a small part of the business."

"That's very commendable, ma'am."

"Um, and it taught me a valuable lesson. Start small, and earn people's trust," said the mistress, as she squeezed Liza's hand.

"Another thing that shaped Papa was that, just like his father, he was fascinated by the sea. He began learning as much as possible about the shipping functions of Mr. Picard's enterprise. I don't want to risk boring you though, Liza, with endless details of Father's life."

"No, ma'am, please! It's like a good story."

"Indeed! But suffice it to say, that Papa went on to become a merchant of high regard and a ship-owner. Along the way, Daddy discovered a stunningly beautiful girl named Rebecca Bradley, working in a dry goods store. Mother came from a family of decent, honest folk who couldn't give a hoot about social pretenses."

"I believe I sensed that in your mother when we met, ma'am," Liza said with a smile.

"That's Momma! So now, let's jump ahead to when I first met Mr. Cauley."

Liza smiled, and eased herself a bit farther onto the bed.

"We were introduced at the home of our dear friends, the Whitmores, of Salisbury, Maryland. I was there for several days' visit at Lucy Whitmore's invitation. Mr. Cauley was a friend of Lucy's brother, Stewart. Lucy knew right away, so she claims, that there was real potential for a relationship between Mr. Cauley and me."

Liza whispered with delight, "It is so wonderful to hear of your romance, Mistress!"

"Well, just wait! You see, the norm for William's visits with Stewart was for them to spend their days mucking about hunting waterfowl or fishing, return just in time to repair for dinner, and then tediously discuss politics all evening with whomever would oblige.

"But on the occasion of my visit, William was apparently . . . *distracted* from his normal pursuits. There was a moment at dinner, in fact, when Stewart actually asked William whether he was ill. I can still see Lucy raising a napkin just in time to avoid relinquishing part of her meal, and then asking to be excused from table."

"Did she suspect the truth, Mistress?"

"Oh yes. I excused myself, too, and when I caught up with Lucy, I asked what had provoked her?"

"What did she say?"

"She said, 'My dear girl, I'm not provoked, but amused beyond measure. Don't you see? William is not physically ill. Rather, he is on the verge of being smitten by affection!'"

"What did you say then, Mistress?"

"Well, I was still unable to imagine that I would be the object of Mr. Cauley's passion. So I asked, 'Pray tell, who is the fortunate young lady?'

"Then Lucy said, 'She may not be fully a lady yet, but if the current course continues, Isabel, you soon *shall* be!'"

"Oh, Mistress, that is so wonderful!"

"Yes! But Lucy's comment both delighted and bewildered me. And that is my point in telling you all of this. I had so much to learn about society! Can you imagine how I felt as we approached that imposing estate of William's parents in Staunton for the very first time?"

"How did you manage it, mistress?"

"I really couldn't. But," Mrs. Cauley said, pointing upward and smiling, "God had a plan. To my great relief, Father Cauley immediately beamed at me during our introduction."

"I don't think that he's ever stopped, Mistress."

"I believe you're right, dear," Mrs. Cauley said with a smile. "And by the time that three day visit at Staunton waned, Mother Cauley was beginning to take me into her confidence."

"But weren't you frightened, at first, about how they would judge you?"

"I was completely unnerved! At dinner the first night, there were *eleven* pieces of silverware at each place setting.

For a girl who learned to shuck oysters with her father's pocketknife, that array of utensils was bewildering."

"What did you do, ma'am?"

"I smiled politely, and picked up whatever piece of silver William's mother did. I watched what she was eating with it, and did the same. That's how you learn, through observation. And that's why I'm so glad that you've taken so to reading, Liza. Books allow us to observe far more than we could ever learn by doing in a lifetime."

"But, mistress, even with observing and learning, when do you stop feeling awkward, and out of place?"

"That can only happen when you learn to accept yourself, Liza."

"But how can I, mistress?"

"By remembering that God loves you. He made you, just as you are, to his great delight! Let his love and his joy radiate through your beautiful face, my dear. Obey him, and trust that he will bless, provide for, guide and protect you."

"Will he always, mistress?"

"Yes. For all those who believe and are trusting in him, he will always do those things, regardless of our circumstances. Remember, Liza, our God is ever faithful."

# Chapter 27

When the new slaves from Mississippi went to Sabbath service for the first time, Essex explained the normal flow of the worship service. Soon Chloe, Lucinda, old Henderson, James, and little Tim were all joyfully singing right along with the others. Of the new slaves, only Chloe's brother, Brister, avoided the Sabbath gathering.

What the newcomers responded to most visibly was the featuring of a personal song, sung by one of the slave family. You could, indeed, have heard a pin drop when Essex stood and said, "Well, for y'all what just come, we been makin' up our own songs ta sing, an' makin' de words come from somethin' in our actual lifes. Mr. Aidan he'p us do dat, cause he have a gif' o' song writin'.

"I done tol' him, in my life, ain't exactly right ta say dat I come *to* de Lawd. I still kain't figure out why, but it were mo' like he actually made de effort ta come ta *me.*"

"Praise God, hallelujah!" the others called out.

"So, me an' Mr. Aidan been workin', good while now, on song called 'In My Savior's Hands.' I'm gettin' kind o' partial to it. Mr. Aidan gwan play de fiddle while I sings. Go somethin' like dis."

## In My Savior's Hands (Slow Tempo)

Oh, ohhhhh, ohh, ohh, ohhhhhh, I-I was
Broken an' hurt
I was drownin' in my sin,
When I felt someone's touch
Turned around an' saw Him.

How he smiled as He wiped de guilt
An' shame right offa' my face,
Den I lookt at His hands
An' I was saved by His grace!

CHORUS

His hands could crush, dey could crush any foe
But dey can dry a little chile's tear,
When dey wrapped around me close I know
I'm beyond any fear.
Now I'm able ta face whatever
Dis world can demand,
In de life-changin' power an' grace I found
In my Savior's hands!

How could we nail dese hands
To a old rugged limb?
D'ese hands dat so humbly washt all dose
Dat shoulda been washin' Him?

D'ese hands dat healed, an' gave faith 'n hope
To de sick ones an' de lame,
D'ese hands dat stayed nailed up dere on dat
ol cross
Till my sins all washt away!

*CHORUS* *His hands could crush, dey could crush any foe*
*But dey can dry a little chile's tear,*
*When dey wrapped around me close I know*
*I'm beyond any fear.*
*Now I'm able ta face whatever*
*Dis world can demand,*
*In de life-changin' power an' grace I found*
*In my Savior's hands!*

By the time Essex began the final chorus, everyone was on their feet, clapping to the beat and praising God as they sang right along with him.

Of course, the first run-through was not nearly enough. Each time the song was repeated, the singers became more familiar with the lyrics and started to anticipate favorite lines and phrases like, "should'a been washin' Him." The reveling went on for more than twenty minutes. When it finally did subside, the Lord had been truly praised and worshiped.

The worship also served to welcome the new slaves, and create a bond with them as an important, new part of life at High Meadows.

# Chapter 28

The week after the new slaves first worshiped under the great oak, Auntie Dee took Chloe with her to the forge. The visit had to be somewhat rushed, as it came in the midst of a very busy workday.

"Gal, hurry an' tell Mr. Aidan here what yuh done tol' me!" Auntie Dee said.

Aidan could sense that Chloe was quite nervous and hesitant to speak. So, he offered, "Please, Chloe, say whatever ye want to say. It's all right."

"W-well, sir..."

"Please call me Aidan."

"Da's *Mister* Aidan," Auntie Dee corrected.

"Well, Mister Aidan, I were tellin' Auntie dat I liked Essex's song ya helped him make. And I tol' her I wisht I could make a song about what happen ta me fo' I got here."

"That's wonderful, Chloe. I would be glad ta help."

"But Mr. Aidan,'" Chloe said uneasily, "my story real *personal.*"

"A personal story makes for a powerful song," Aidan said, "because it makes the song real." Still, he could sense that she was very hesitant to share any of the details of it.

"Think about this, then, Chloe. If ye decide ta work at the song with me, I promise not ta share a bit of it with any other livin' soul, except Auntie. She should come sit with us when you're here. Then after awhile, *you* can decide whether ye want ta share your song with anyone else."

"I still ain't sure, Mr. Aidan," Chloe said, looking down at her feet.

"That's fine. But I can tell ye this, Chloe. If it's about something that still bothers you, somethin' that ye think about and it makes ye sad over and over again, makin' the song and singin' it can help ye feel better. It's a way of bringin' out the pain that is way down deep inside of you, and then lettin' it all go."

Auntie elbowed Chloe, who responded by asking, "Can I think on it?"

"Of course," he assured her.

"All right, Mr. Aidan," Auntie speculated, "I say she gwan t'ink ta *do* it!"

As Auntie and Chloe left the forge, Aidan's heart ached for the girl. Her's was obviously a hurt that ran deeply. But as Aidan hoped for Chloe to return, a request for him to help with another song came from Ursule, the seamstress.

"Mr. Aidan," she said one day after worship, "what if we has a idea for a song dat ain't really about us?"

"What is it about, Ursule?"

"It about Jesus—how he is and what he done for us."

"I can't think of a better thing to sing about."

"Well, dis about my favorite Bible story. I ain't heard ya preach on it, but I figures ya knows about it jus' de same. It de story 'bout a woman who have a problem none o' de doctahs could fix."

"Except for the great doctor, right?"

"See, I knew you heard it!"

"And it should make a wonderful song, Ursule," Aidan joyfully assured her.

# Chapter 29

Mr. Cauley's stallion was a bit labored in its gait after the master returned one day from Richmond. Aidan took a closer look at the horse's hooves and saw some gaps in how the shoes fit. It turned out that the smith who shod the animal while Mr. Cauley was away did not 'hot forge' the shoes.

So the master agreed to let Aidan put the horse right. After feeling the difference Aidan's work made in his steed, Mr. Cauley returned to the forge to thank Aidan.

"You've done fine work!" proclaimed Mr. Cauley as he entered. "Orion feels like his old self again. I thought he was just worn down from our journey. But now he's sound as a dollar!"

Aidan replied, "You are more than welcome, sir. I don't want to criticize the other smith, but I've always felt hot forgin's the only way ta go, smoke and all."

"I am pleased with your efforts, Aidan. And the mistress appreciates what you've done to make improvements at the manse."

"Thank you, sir. And . . . "

"What is it, Aidan?"

"I wondered if I could ask a bit of a favor, sir?"

"Why yes, what is it?"

"It is for me boy's benefit."

At this, the master playfully patted Jack on the belly and said, "If there is a way I can help this young smith's apprentice, I'd welcome it, I'm sure."

"Well then, I know, sir, that the Cauley family is a distinguished clan that is important in Virginia and throughout all the country. Could you share with us some of the grand things that your family has done?"

"My good man," the master chuckled, "you never have to bend a politician's arm to get him to speak! The only question," he said, as he motioned for them to sit while he perched on an empty barrel, "is where to start?

"Well, I suppose I inherited my taste for the political life from my father, and he in turn, from his father. Both were members of the Virginia Assembly, and Grandfather was well-known among our nation's founding fathers.

"Cauleys have also shed blood and risked life for family and country against the French, Indians, and the British.

Our relatives served with distinction at the Battle of Yorktown where the British commander, Cornwallis, surrendered to George Washington. That eventually secured our nation's independence from the British."

"I see, sir!" Aidan said with great admiration.

"We are equally proud," the master continued, "to hail from Virginia, the birthplace of so many of our nation's leaders. Thomas Jefferson penned much of the Declaration of Independence, and James Madison played a similar role in creating our US Constitution. They, and four other Virginians have gone on to become presidents of the United States. Both Jefferson and Madison visited our home more than once when I was a boy.

"And I remember Father speaking so highly of Patrick Henry. I believe he died just before I was born. But we learned about him in school. He, as much as any man, urged us to fight for freedom when he uttered those immortal words, 'Give me liberty, or give me death!'"

"And if you don't mind me observing, sir," Aidan ventured, "he bore a good Irish name."

"You're right, Aidan. And he had the fire to match!"

Jack asked, "What were those founder fathers like, sir?"

The master smiled. "Well Mother, like most women who knew him, always spoke rather dreamily about Jefferson's charming and elegant manners. I often heard Madison described as being quite a sharp, shrewd man. And he was a little fellow, nearly a foot shorter than George Washington! Washington, of course, was our first president. He died around the same time as Patrick Henry, so I never met him. But my father told me about seeing President Washington for the first time, when Father was about your age, Jack. He said he would never forget how tall, strong, and fearless George looked. To father, it appeared as though the many brass buttons on the front of the president's waistcoat, indeed, reached halfway to the sky!"

"Oh my!" Jack said with delight.

Sensing that this had already been a kind effort on the master's part to enlighten them, Aidan asked, "Could you help us understand one more thing, sir?"

"Certainly, Aidan."

"I've heard that slaves, or servants, enjoy much more hospitable treatment up here in the Virginia Valley, than those in the Deep South. I am sure for us, sir, that is much due to your and Mrs. Cauley's kindness."

"Why thank you, Aidan."

"Yes, sir. But why would that also be true in a general sense?"

"Well, some would actually question that, Aidan. Regretfully, abuse of servants still occurs in these environs. Generally, though, you can make a case for better treatment here, and some of that has to do with our mainstay crop—wheat. It requires far less labor. We plant it, pray for rain, and harvest it. There is less need to drive workers hard than there is raising cotton or tobacco, because those crops must be cultivated throughout the growing season. And the increased labor is made even more brutal by the intense heat they have further south. Lastly, and most regrettably, I have observed that once someone crosses the line of abusing another human being, they are far more likely to repeat it, and to do so in ever harsher degrees."

"Well, thank you, sir," Aidan said solemnly, as Mr. Cauley stood to take his leave.

Just then, to Aidan's embarrassment, Jack chirped, "Could you come back tomorrow, sir, and tell us about fightin' the Indians?"

The master chuckled and said, "Well, I didn't fight the Indians myself, Jack."

Then Mr. Cauley looked thoughtfully at the boy for a moment and said, "But I can tell you an interesting story about someone who both fought, and was greatly admired by the Indians."

After the master retook is perch upon the barrel, Jack and Aidan sat spellbound while Mr. Cauley explained, "Before we fought for independence against the British, they occupied us as our colonial sovereign. And at that time, George Washington actually aided the British forces in their ongoing conflict with the French.

"The French controlled much of what was known as the Ohio Country from their headquarters at Fort Duquesne in Pittsburgh.

"Washington was assigned to aid General Edward Braddock, who commanded an expeditionary force of over two thousand men. Their goal was to engage and defeat the French at Fort Duquesne, then go on to destroy the French stronghold on the Great Lakes at Fort Niagara.

"The French enlisted the aid of hundreds of native Indians, Jack, in their fight. They joined with troops led by a young French officer who pleaded with his commander at Fort Duquesne for a chance to go out to meet General Braddock in the wilderness. He felt their smaller force would stand a better chance by striking at Braddock with a surprise attack.

"They surprised the British, indeed, with a deadly barrage of fire from both sides. Chaos reigned! General Braddock and his officers served with great valor in rallying their troops to stand and fight. But they couldn't even see their clever French and Indian enemies, who hunkered down in ditches and behind trees, as they blasted away at the bright, red coats of the British.

"Colonel George Washington was only twenty-three years old at the time. And despite the fact that he'd been perilously ill for ten days, Washington's valor was widely acknowledged. He did his best to carry out the general's commands amongst the thundering barrage of French and Indian muskets.

"The young colonel was in particular danger because, like all officers, he carried out his duties from horseback. Indian braves were directly ordered to shoot anyone on a horse first. And they had special orders to kill the tall, young warrior Washington. Their chief recognized that George was shrewd, and was encouraging his men to fight the same, stealthful way that the Indians did.

"But no matter how many times they fired, their guns couldn't strike Washington. In the course of trying, they shot two horses right out from under him!"

Jack whistled in amazement.

"Then General Braddock was mortally wounded. He would die in retreat three days later. In all, more than seven hundred British and American soldiers were killed or wounded in The Battle of Monongahela. By all accounts, only one officer was still on horseback at the battle's end—George Washington."

Then Mr. Cauley leaned forward to make a point. "The day immediately following the fight, Washington made an amazing discovery. He found four bullet holes shot right through his coat! Miraculously, he hadn't suffered a scratch.

"I've told you all of this for a reason, Aidan and Jack. You see, fifteen years after the battle, Washington visited the site of the conflict while looking at some land in the area. News of Washington's visit spread to Indians who had taken part in the battle. Their now elderly chief traveled a considerable distance to see and meet with his former enemy, the brave, young warrior.

"The chief held a tribal council meeting for the occasion. Through an interpreter, he told his former advisary that he had personally shot to kill Washington, eighteen times! Then he ordered his braves to *stop shooting* at George, because he was obviously a favorite of heaven! The chief also prophesized, correctly, that the tall, young officer would one day lead a great nation."

Jack and Aidan just shook their heads in awe.

The master concluded in a very inspiring tone, "The story I have just told you has been verified to the point that it is now a part of the schoolbooks of instruction in the history of these United States. May the children of America always be taught, just how richly God has blessed us."

# Chapter 30

Master Cauley left once again for Richmond. The following night, an event occurred around midnight that shook High Meadows to its very core. Aidan first learned of it when Auntie Dee appeared at the door of the forge dressed in her night robe.

"Mr. Aidan! Mr. Aidan! Open up!"

Aidan pulled on trousers, went to the door and asked Auntie to step in.

"What is it, Auntie Dee?"

"Slabes, come. Dey's runaways!"

"Where, Auntie Dee?"

"Got 'em hid in de kitchen. Fo' o' dem. Said dey heard 'bout our new slabes gwan hab better life up here. So dey start followin' along out o' sight behind de mastah. Den dey gets lost. Den dey was picked up by de un'erground railroad. Conductor come. Lef' 'em in de woods obuh yonder."

"All right, Auntie Dee. Give me just a moment," Aidan said, as he struggled to clear his head and begin to craft a plan.

Then he said, "I think you should go back and keep them quiet. Keep your lamp low. I'll have Liza waken the mistress, and someone will come to speak to them soon. Just pray and stay calm."

"I can do de *prayin'* part, Mr. Aidan," Auntie said. "Calm I ain't shuh 'bout."

Aidan entered the main house and asked young Timothy, who slept just inside the back door, to summon Liza. In turn, Liza brought the mistress down within minutes.

"What is it, Aidan? Has someone taken ill?" Mrs. Cauley asked.

Aidan checked to see that Timothy had returned to his bed, then spoke softly. "No, ma'am. Auntie Dee just came to me and said that four runaway slaves have arrived here from Mississippi. It appears they heard your new servants would have it much better here, so they ran away and found their way to us."

The mistress quickly sat down and held both hands to her heart.

"Why, this situation is impossible! Dear Lord, what shall we do?"

"If I may, ma'am," Aidan offered, "I've had a few minutes to consider."

"Of course, Aidan; what are your ideas?"

"Two choices came to mind, ma'am. They could be held here and their owner notified."

"I hate to think of the consequences for them," the mistress said nervously.

"Yes, or they could be held here, in secret, till we figure where they can safely go."

Liza's face showed agreement with that thought as she suggested, "They could go on up North, ma'am."

"But what if we're found out first?" cried the mistress. Lowering her voice again, she fairly shook as she said, "It would *ruin* William. Why, he might even face criminal charges!"

"Yes, ma'am," Aidan acknowledged. "That is why we would need to find a very safe hiding place, then move quickly to get them on their way again."

"Where would you hide them?" asked Liza. "There are some hereabouts who can't know the slaves are with us."

"Yes, Aidan, where would they be safe?" the mistress asked.

"I was makin' repairs last month down inside the ice-house, ma'am. The earthen wall gave way and revealed a small passageway. It looked like pretty tight goin' so I didn't explore it—just placed heavy timbers over the opening. But I could go further back in and see if it opens up to a larger cave."

"Of course, these hills are riddled with caverns," Mrs. Cauley acknowledged.

Then Aidan suggested, "We could keep the runaways in Auntie's food larder for now. Tomorrow, I'll appear ta be checkin' on the repairs I made, then reopen the passageway ta see whether there's enough space beyond ta house them."

"I hate to think what might be lurking in a hole like that, that could harm them," Mrs. Cauley cautioned.

"I'll go back in with a torch and see if there's enough air-flow, and make sure it's safe."

"Well, if your foray tomorrow still makes you think this would be our most favorable course, then agreed. Liza, it will cause less suspicion if you go alone to talk to Auntie Dee, now. Tell her they should stay with her until tomorrow night. Tell her they must stay still back in the larder, and remain silent!"

"Yes, ma'am, right away."

Then Aidan said, "Thank you, Mrs. Cauley."

"Why do you thank me, Aidan?"

"For givin' these poor souls a fightin' chance, ma'am."

# Chapter 31

The next morning, Aidan asked Liza to occupy Jack as he descended into the icehouse with hand tools and a torch.

Aidan had never seen one of these structures back home in Ireland. On the surface, the High Meadows icehouse looked like a stubby shed with walls only about four feet tall. It was sixteen feet square with a peaked roof. Inside lay a deep, cylindrical chamber that could hold layer upon layer of ice, separated by buffers of insulating straw. Empty, as the icehouse nearly was now, the hole was about eighteen feet deep. Aidan reached the bottom by a wooden ladder built into the wall beside a loading platform operated by block and tackle.

When he reopened the cave passageway, a musty dampness engulfed him. As Aidan began to crawl with a torch into the opening, the first few feet required him to twist and turn.

After crawling back eight or ten feet, his spirit soared to see a much larger opening straight ahead! There was a small pool of water directly in front of him that seemed to be run off from the melting ice. But the larger room was elevated a bit, and it was dry.

Once he reached the middle of it, Aidan could stand and actually had trouble reaching the peak of the roof with the torch. He noticed that the flame began to waver in a gentle updraft. There had to be a crevice to the surface above. That meant the slaves would be able to burn a torch for some warmth and comfort, and not be choked by the smoke. But Aidan reckoned it would be best to burn torches only at night, so telltale smoke wouldn't be seen up above. Candlelight would have to do during the day.

Aidan made a mental note of the size and shape of the cave, and calculated that it would more than accommodate the group of runaways. There were plenty of spots to lie down and rest. A passageway continued from the far end of the room. As Aidan explored it, he realized this space could serve as a privy for the slaves. He went a bit farther and used a pry bar to dig a ditch latrine.

Aidan retraced his steps and carefully replaced the timbers over the opening. Then he returned to Jack and Liza where he'd left them on the back porch of the manse.

Jack protested, "You're not here to fetch me already, are you, Papa? Miss Liza isn't done showing me how to make a tail for a kite!"

"That sounds a useful skill, Jack," Aidan said, "but Miss Liza and we have much work that needs tendin'. Liza, can we work with you on makin' a kite tail, and a kite to tie it to, soon?"

"Of course," she said with a smile, as she studied Aidan's face for a hint of what he had discovered.

"Good.  And while I think of it, please tell the mistress that the repairs in the icehouse looked fine.  Tell her, too, that there's plenty o' room for storage down there now."

# Chapter 32

About mid-morning, while she nervously went about her duties with her kitchen larder full of runaway slaves, Auntie Dee had the fright of her life. She looked up from kneading dough to see Phineas Snead standing in her doorway!

Auntie clutched her breast and said, "Lawd, Mr. Snead, yuh gave me such a fright!"

Snead insinuated, "Why, do you have something to hide?"

"Yuh knows Auntie Dee, Mister Snead. What yuh sees is what yuh gets! Why has yuh come dis mo'nin'?"

It was all Auntie Dee could do to stay composed as she wondered if Snead had already found out about the slaves she was hiding. But Snead's suspicions proved to be no more than his usual unpleasantness, as he sheepishly muttered, "I have a damn boil been bothering me. Can you make something to draw it out?"

"Let me see it."

"Can't," said Snead in disgust.

"Why's dat, Mr. Snead?" Auntie Dee asked playfully.

"Let's just say it hurts to sit down."

Trying not to laugh, Auntie Dee couldn't suppress a little snort that she quickly covered up with a cough.

"Well," she said, "dat mean yuh bes' spend some time layin' on yuh belly. How long yuh had it?"

"About a week."

"Yuh can draw it out in a day or two wit' dis," Auntie said as she handed Snead a large onion. "Slice it, an' put de fresh cut part where it hurt. Cover it wit' a cloth yuh soaks in hot water from off de stove. Lay down an' don't get up fuh a hour. Do dat couple, t'ree time a day, an' it'a draw out an' start ta drain. Don't try'n coax it out on yuh own or de infection gwan spread. Dat when it get real bad an' yuh gits carbuncle."

"How am I supposed to run this place and lay about for two days?"

"Kain't he'p dat, Mr. Snead. But if yuh wants get bettuh, I done tol' yuh what fuh do."

"I'll put on your remedy when I retire, along with enough bourbon to make me sleep."

"Da's prob'ly de best cure o' all!" Auntie said, instantly realizing the benefit of having Snead groggy from drink the night the slaves had to be moved.

"Humph!" Snead snorted, as he snatched the onion, turned and left.

Auntie gave out a deep sigh, looked at the larder door and whispered, "Oh t'ank yuh, Lawd Jesus, fuh keepin' 'em quiet."

As Auntie began to settle into her dough kneading again, Liza arrived to deliver the same message she had just shared with Aidan.

"Auntie Dee, good morning," Liza said, with a sense of urgency.

"Sumpin' wrong, Liza?" Auntie wondered.

Liza whispered, "No, but I have instructions from the mistress. She doesn't want us to move the slaves tonight until she is sure all are asleep at the manse. Then she'll move a lighted candle to her bedchamber window on this side, where you and Aidan can see it. She'll hold it there for just a moment, then blow out the flame.

# Chapter 33

It seemed to Aidan like half the night had already passed when he finally saw a candle briefly appear, and be blown out at Mrs. Cauley's bedchamber window. It was, in fact, just after midnight.

Soon Auntie Dee, Liza, and the four slaves arrived at the door of the forge. "Dis'll hold 'em fuh day or two," Auntie said, as she handed Aidan a large basket of food and candles. "An' Essex keepin' de dogs all quiet, out at de barn," she assured.

Liza and the slaves carried bedding. In addition to Auntie's basket, Aidan toted a pair of unlit torches.

A quarter moon shone a soft light as Aidan, Liza and the slaves crept alongside the shrubbery behind the mansion. Their hearts raced when they had to scurry, fully exposed, across the lawn to the icehouse.

Aidan went first and led Liza down the slippery, wooden ladder into the darkened pit. A smoky, gray wisp of moonlight from the doorway above cast an eerie mist above them. Once down the ladder, Aidan lit a candle and handed it to Liza. Then he climbed back up to assist the frightened party as they backed into the open door, felt for the top ladder rung with their feet, and carefully descended. Once the slaves were safely on the floor, Aidan closed the door and clambered down to join them.

Then he lit a torch. The slaves' shivering faces, pulsing in the torch light, ingrained an image Aidan couldn't forget. "Don't worry," he said, as he tried to comfort them. "You don't have ta stay here in the cold." Then he told a tall, young male, "Hold this," as he handed him the torch.

Aidan labored quickly to remove the timbers and reveal the passageway. Then he lit the second torch from the first and said, "Follow me." Soon he and Liza had the slaves settled in their hiding place.

Aidan instructed them, "Never speak above a whisper in here. Only burn a torch at night, so no smoke will be spotted up above during the day. I'll leave the timbers lying loose across the opening to the cave, so you can see daylight from above. Then you'll know when to put the torches out. Only use the candles during the day.

"We will try to return each night, to bring food and check on you until we can get you on your way. Take a torch farther back the passage. You'll see I dug a privy ditch there. You will not be staying here long. We plan ta move you up North, to freedom. Is there anythin' ye want ta say?"

Their faces showed hints of gratitude, but not full trust. No one spoke.

"I want ta pray for you, then, before we go. What are your names?"

"No!" cried Liza. Then she whispered, "Don't ask that."

The insistence in her voice made Aidan not question her. So he quickly prayed a short prayer for their general safety. Then he and Liza left.

They met Auntie Dee, who had stayed by Jack's side in the event he should wake. Relieved to hear how things had gone, Auntie informed them, "Conductor be here fuh dem tumahruh night. So our work done."

Aidan asked, "Should I be ready to show the conductor where they are?"

"No, Mr. Aidan!" Auntie Dee insisted. "Conductor already *know* where dey is. Don't need yuh he'p now."

Then Auntie quickly said good-night and returned to her quarters.

Liza looked at Aidan sympathetically and said, "I am sorry I shouted at you about not asking the slaves their names. You don't want to know, because if slave hunters come, they won't be able to get the names out of you. And forget their faces, and how light or dark their skin was. Just forget everything about them."

"But how did Auntie find out about the conductor?" he asked.

"You don't want to know that, either. Just trust they will handle it all from here. I must go now. Good-night, Aidan,"

Liza said, as she gently squeezed his arm and disappeared into the night.

He closed the door after Liza, then slumped onto his cot. Aidan was grateful that Jack had not stirred all evening. But his thoughts and emotions were churning at this sudden turn of events. Earlier, he was feeling good about doing his part to help the runaways. Now, though, he felt like no more than a bit player in a mysterious and very deadly game—a game in which he was struggling, just to learn the rules.

# Chapter 34

The night when the slaves were to be picked up by the underground conductor, Aidan labored to calm his mind and fall asleep. He knew that trying to observe what was going on would only put everyone involved at risk.

Sometime well past midnight he finally succumbed to fatigue. But he felt sure he'd heard no hint of the slaves' departure, prior to drifting off.

At first light, it was all he could do to keep from plunging down the icehouse ladder to check whether the slaves had gone, and to see if the passageway had been properly boarded up. But here, again, Aidan knew it would be better not to risk raising suspicion. Instead, he paid an early visit to Auntie Dee. He found her in a particularly joyous mood.

"Dere yuh is, Mr. Aidan, jus' de bery soul I been t'inkin' on!"

"Why, good morning, Auntie Dee. How so?"

"So's I can git yuh he'p makin' Auntie's song all nice an' pretty, jus' like yuh done dem udder ones."

"You have an idea for a song, Auntie Dee?"

"Shuh do, Mr. Aidan. Got me a song o' praise I wants ta sing, cause de Lawd make all t'ings turn out right fuh his surbants in de end," Auntie said, nodding her head in the direction of the icehouse.

Catching her clue, and relieved to know that the slaves made it out all right, Aidan said, "Amen, amen! Auntie Dee, do you have any words set for your song?"

"Shuh do. Start like dis, 'I sing my praises to yuh, Lawd, I jumps right up an' shouts; cause yuh de only one I knows, I really wanna shout about!'"

"I like it already, Auntie! When did it come to you?"

"I figure 'twas 'bout two o'clock in de mo'nin', Mr. Aidan," Auntie said with a wink. Then she laughed and said, "Yuh know, we used ta call dat time o' night 'hagholluh' down de' lowlands."

"What does that mean?" Aidan wondered.

"Oh, jus' part o' dem ol' ways, Mr. Aidan, 'bout believin' in spirits an' such. Hags s'posed ta be witches dat come out afta' midnight, 'holluh', an' make scary noise. Up here d'ough, gits awful quiet 'round den. Real good time ta t'ink," she whispered, "an' listen."

Smiling broadly, Aidan said, "I see. That's a colorful expression. But I'm like you, Auntie. I like the new ways much better. If you'll sing your song's first lines again a time or two, I'll get the melody down. But first, what else do you want the song ta say?"

"I wants folk ta know how God made Auntie Dee all brand new. He take all my fears an' sorrows, an' throw'd 'em out like bunch o' dirty ol' rags. Den he give me real peace inside, an' joy!"

"Yes," Aidan agreed. "We are made new creatures in him. The old nature passes away, and we are transformed by the renewin' of our minds."

"You right dere, Mr. Aidan. An' I don't mean sound like I's no'mannus. But I don't want dis here song comin' out like no crickety ol' chu'ch tune. Dis here hab ta be *Auntie's* kind o' wuhship—singin', jumpin', shoutin' fuh joy!"

"Just like when we get ta glory, Auntie!"

"Amen on dat! An' ain't it sumpin', Mr. Aidan?"

"What's that, Auntie?"

"I reckon dey's some folk we knows gwan reach glory," then she whispered, "in jus' a couple days!"

# Chapter 35

One bright day, Mrs. Cauley decided to provide time for Liza to start to tutor Jack on a regular basis. Under the mistress's teaching, of course, Liza had become refined and educated. Now Mrs. Cauley saw benefit in Liza passing her knowledge along to Aidan's son. And she hoped the experience would prepare Liza to teach the other slaves, if the day came when it would be legal to do so.

Jack spoke fairly well for his age. Aidan humbly gave credit for that to Jack's dear mother. But Liza would go on to teach Jack use of the alphabet, beautiful penmanship, and many new words as well. Eventually, she taught him to put his thoughts together in a way that truly made sense. Aidan was so proud when Jack began to commit a few of those thoughts to paper.

At the end of the workday, Jack and his papa would often go fishing. As things were settling down after the runaway slaves left High Meadows, Aidan gladly consented when Jack asked, "Papa, can we go wet a line?"

He surprised his father, though, as they settled in along the bank of the stream and Jack asked, "Can I ask you a question about Miss Liza?"

"How do you mean, Jack?"

"Well, I know you think she is nice and everything."

"Yes, of course," Aidan said, as he wondered where Jack's young mind was headed.

"But I mean, do you think she is *real* nice?"

"Real nice in what way, son?"

"Oh, I don't know, maybe to have her be with us all the time, like Momma used to be."

"Well!" Aidan exclaimed. "How would *you* feel about that?"

"Mostly, I think it would be good."

"Mostly?"

"Papa, it's not like I don't like it being just you and me all the time, the way we are now. But I still miss Momma."

"I know you do, son. So do I."

"So, I think Momma wouldn't mind it if Miss Liza sort of helped out, to make things nice for us," Jack surmised.

"Um, I agree that Miss Liza would be very good at that. And no, I don't think your Momma would mind it a bit, not now. It's been a long time that we've been missin' her. And she knows that we always will. So it would not be a question of being untrue to her. I'm sure of that, Jack."

"Oh, no!" Jack was quick to agree.

"But this is marriage we're talkin' about, son, and that can be a tricky business."

"What do you mean, Papa?"

"Well, let's look at our situation. We're really talkin' about makin' a whole new family, right?"

"Well, it wouldn't be new for us, just for her."

"Of course. But, in important ways for *all* of us, this would be a new arrangement."

"OK, well maybe a little bit."

"Right. So there would be three people in the new family: you, me, and Miss Liza."

"Right," Jack giggled, "until babies come!"

At that, Aidan dropped his fishing pole, grabbed and tickled his boy and said, "Hold on there, lad. One dad-burned thing at a time! OK," Aidan continued, as he picked up his pole, "at the *beginning*, at least, there would be three people. And what we're saying, here, is that *you* think it would be a good idea for us to have a new Mrs. Smith."

"Mm-hmm!"

"And *I've* been thinking it might be a good idea to have a new Mrs. Smith."

"So that just leaves Liza, Papa. Do you want me to ask her tomorrow?"

"No! I mean, it's up ta the man to ask a lady that. Me point, son, which seems ta somehow be gettin' completely lost, is that *Miss Liza* will have ta think that bein' Mrs. Smith is a good idea too—that is, if this whole new arrangement is ta have a real chance of workin' out."

"She likes you, Papa. I can tell."

"And I like her, too. But I think that Miss Liza has some questions about whether it would really be a good idea to be my wife."

"Why's that?"

"Well . . . because we're different. The places we came from are different. Our lives have been very different."

"Is it because we *look* different?" Jack wondered.

"Maybe that's part of it."

"I used to think that, too, Papa. But she really is just like us. She laughs, and tells me stories, and cares about me just like Momma did. And if she had a chance, I think she could even cook like Auntie Dee. Miss Liza is really smart!"

Aidan was beginning to weaken under this relentless barrage of innocent reason. "I am sure you are right about all of that, Jack. But remember, we have ta wait until *Miss Liza* feels that we really are the same. Be patient because . . ."

"I know, Papa. All good things come to those who wait upon the Lord."

"Just look!" Aidan said, as he pointed to Jack's popping cork bobber out in the stream.

"You've got a bite!"

# Chapter 36

Aidan was anxious to share from the Book of Genesis about the creation of the world the next Sabbath morning. But as the slaves walked down from the quarter to the great oak tree, he noticed that one of their number was missing, Chloe. And he saw one new face, that of an older gentleman standing with Liza.

"Mr. Aidan Smith, please allow me to introduce my father, Mr. Walter Moore. Daddy, this is Mr. Aidan Smith," Liza said with her usual grace.

"Mr. Moore, how do you do?" Aidan said as he extended his hand to meet Mr. Moore's.

"Hello, Mr. Aidan. My Liza mention you to me often. Pleased likewise. Uh, would y'all mind if I sits down?"

"Please do, Mr. Moore," Aidan said. "We should be ready to start soon."

Aidan, Jack and the Moores sat together on the first log of their brush arbor church. Though in this case, that description might be a misnomer. Many slave worship and meeting places were located out in the brush or swamps, well out of ear shot of masters that the slaves prayed to be delivered from. "Lord, send us a Moses!" was the common cry. But at High Meadows, the worship site was simply chosen as the place that provided the most shade.

As often was the case, this Sunday's service began with rounds of spontaneous singing of songs like "Hold On," "Ain't That Good News," "Open the Window, Noah," "By and By," "O'er the Crossin'," and "Get Away, Jordan." As one well-loved song of praise waned, someone would start the first line of another. The singing involved much more repetition than Aidan and Jack had been used to back home. But they grew to appreciate this new style of having a "caller" lead, and everyone else respond or "base" the song.

Some whites disparaged this singing style as a sign that slaves were incapable of remembering lyrics, and needed a caller to remind them. But because it was against the law to teach a slave to read, Aidan knew these criticisms were unfair. He wondered, *"How many white congregations, without bein' able ta read from a hymnal, could recite all the verses without error?"*

After half an hour or so of singing praises, it came time for the message.

Aidan drew up his most prized possession, a well-worn copy of the Word. He opened it to chapter one of Genesis and shared, "This past week, during a quiet time with the Lord, he seemed ta speak to me heart about a new course ta take in our readin'."

"Hmm?" the group wondered in anticipation.

"He seemed ta encourage me ta begin at the beginnin'—with the book of Genesis."

"Sound fine, Mr. Aidan. Read on!" someone called out.

Aidan soon came to the passage, "And God said, 'Let the earth bring forth grass, the herb yielding seed, and the fruit tree yielding fruit after his kind, whose seed is in itself, upon the earth: and it was so.

And the earth brought forth grass, and herb yielding seed after his kind, and the tree yielding fruit, whose seed was in itself, after his kind: and God saw that it was good.'"

As he finished reading, Aidan asked, "Was there anythin' that stood out ta anyone in that passage?"

After a little hesitation, Liza offered, "Why no, Mr. Aidan, other than the awesome wonder of God's great creation."

Her comment drew agreement and spurred others to speak as well.

Then Aidan had a joyous announcement.

"We have special music again this Sabbath day! Ursule is going ta grace us with a song about one of her favorite stories from the Bible."

The loving slave family welcomed and encouraged Ursule, as she straightened her straw hat and made her way to stand before them.

She giggled and said, "Any y'all heard me sing knows, singin' ain't my gif'." That brought laughter. "But I loves my Lawd and Savior."

"Mm-hmm!"

"So I make dis song fo' him, 'bout someone in de Bible who have faith I wisht I could git. Song called, 'When Jesus Came A-Walkin,' and Mr. Aidan say it all right ta say it dat way." That brought more laughter.

"An' even d'ough dis song 'bout a woman's kind o' problem, de tune of it end up bein' sumpin' dat maybe chillun wanna sing. So all y'all li'l ones, come on up front an' watch me close, so's ya can sing de part about Jesus."

Little Lucy, Laney, Jack and Dan quickly gathered at Ursule's feet.

Then she said, "All right, here we go!"

Ursule's face took on an animated expression as Aidan introduced the song on the fiddle with a light, pluckish flair. The audience immediately began to pat out the song's rhythm on their laps or log seats. Then Ursule captivated them with this familiar Bible story.

*When Jesus Came A-Walkin' (Mid Tempo)*

*Dey's a story in de Bible*
*Somewhares in de Book of Mark,*
*Ain't a story 'bout Elijah*
*Or ol Noah an' his ark.*

*Dis a story 'bout a woman*
*Who been sufferin' mighty bad,*
*All de doctahs couldn't he'p her*
*But dey took all dat she had.*

Then Ursule beckoned to the children to sing along with her:

*CHORUS (starts slowly, then builds to racing tempo)*
*But when Jesus came a-walkin'*
*Dat poor woman's healin' come,*
*If only she could touch His coat*
*Her sufferin' would be done.*
*She squeeze 'tween da disciples*
*An' she lightly brush His cloak,*
*Den all her sorrows disappear*
*Jus' like a puff of smoke!*

*(dramatically here)*
*But Jesus know some power*
*Have gone out from what she done,*
*He turn an' say "who touch me?"*
*Till dat woman finally come!*

*She scared but tell Him tru'ful*
*Standing', shaking' like a leaf,*
*Till Jesus say "My daughter*
*Your strong faith have set you free!"*

*CHORUS (starts slowly then builds to racing tempo)*
*But when Jesus came a-walkin'*
*Dat poor woman's healin' come,*
*If only she could touch His coat*
*Her sufferin' would be done.*
*She squeeze 'tween da disciples*
*An' she lightly brush His cloak,*
*Den all her sorrows disappear*
*Jus' like a puff of smoke!*

Each time she started the chorus, Ursule slowly walked in place and built up the pace by swinging her arms as the song's tempo quickened. The children all giggled, then screamed with delight, as they swung their arms faster and faster.

The song was met with raucous praise and applause. And Ursule had to consent to several encores in response to shouts of, "You ain't done, gal. Sing it again!"

As the congregation finally dismissed with hearts uplifted, Liza turned to Aidan and said, "I've made a little picnic. If Daddy can tolerate it, I thought we'd stroll down to the stream. We'd enjoy it even more if you and Jack could join us."

Overhearing Liza, Jack nearly wiggled out of his skin before Aidan could say, "We'd be delighted!"

After a stop at the manse, Aidan carried a well-laden basket as Liza steadied her father on her arm.

"Y'all has it real nice here, ya know," observed Mr. Moore.

"We know, Daddy. But thank you for reminding."

"And what about you, Mr. Aidan? Will you be stayin' here for good?"

"For the next nine years, at least, Mr. Moore. I have a servitude to finish."

"Hmm. That may sound like a long time to a young man. But I trust it will pass quickly."

"Thank you, sir, for that wish."

Mr. Moore almost seemed to startle at being addressed as "sir." But as Aidan gazed upon this once strong man, bent with years of hard labor, he had the deepest respect for Liza's father.

When they reached a shaded, grassy spot near the stream's edge, Liza began a magic practiced by skilled, feminine hands through the ages. In just moments, she presented a rustic feast that Aidan gladly dedicated with a blessing.

Then he commented, "Oh, my! Did Auntie Dee prepare all this?"

"Why no," Liza said, with a hint of indignation. "I had a little extra time on my *own* hands."

"Papa!" Jack chirped, "See, I told you!"

"Told you what, Aidan?" Liza asked with piqued interest.

Aidan hesitated, to gather his thoughts. "Well . . . I am amazed, but not *surprised* at your skill, Miss Liza. And Jack did speculate that if you wanted, you could cook, (now whispering) just as good as Auntie."

Mr. Moore chuckled and said, "You *bes'* not say that too loud, now! But my baby sure can cook, jus' like her Momma."

"Oh, Daddy, hush!" protested Liza.

They all sat in the grassy shade and thoroughly enjoyed a wonderful meal of baked ham, parsleyed potatoes, sweet pea salad, corn bread, peach cobbler, and cool lemonade.

Then Jack ran and fetched fishing poles, so he and Mr. Moore could try their hand at the stream. Aidan helped Liza repack all but a little "pickin' food" for later. He used their time alone to ask Liza about her parents' life together.

"Momma and Daddy had a special kind of love," Liza began. "He was so strong, and she always looked like a young girl in his arms. Daddy was never afraid to show affection in front of us, though there were times it did embarrass Momma.

"I understand," Aidan said with a smile.

"But she could stand up to his strength, when she had to," Liza insisted.

"What would make her do that?" Aidan asked.

"Oh, disagreements about money and how to use it. Sometimes Daddy would hire out on Sunday afternoons to earn something. Then he'd always want to spend what he earned right away on her or us. Momma insisted they save."

"It sounds like they were very good for each other," Aidan concluded.

"Yes, in many ways, I think they complimented one another.'

"How do you picture them in your mind, when you think of them together, Liza?"

"In front of the fire at the end of a long day as Momma is mending his socks, or patching the knees in his pants. Daddy is smoking his pipe and going on about something he heard someone say, or something he would like to do some day. Momma is rocking, and giving a little wry smile, saying, "Mm-hmm," or just responding with her eyes. I can still see the fire reflected in her eyes."

"That sounds like a home," Aidan sighed.

"Um-hmm," said Liza, as she pretended to be rocking like her momma. They both laughed.

Then Liza said, "Now your turn. Please tell me about your folks."

"Papa looks like me with gray hair, and a little less of it. Me sainted mother put up with all o' us, so that made her turn gray even younger. But she's still pretty in her way. Two brothers—one a smith, one a mason, and three sisters all married."

"That sounds like quite a family! And another blacksmith, too."

"Two more, countin' Papa. That goes back for generations. It's why we have the surname Smith."

"I never heard of that custom. It's charming."

"I wish all me relatives were!" Aidan chucked. "But I miss them just the same. Every day I wonder how they're fairin'. Mr. Cauley posted that letter for me ta home. I wanted ta make sure Louisa's folk knew what happened to her. And I want everyone to know Jack and I are all right. Never heard anythin' back, though."

"Oh you will, Aidan. I'm sure of it. Still, it must be very hard for you and Jack to be separated, so far away from home."

"Yes, but we have ta make this feel like our home now. I'm forbidden ta ever go back ta Ireland again.

"Umm."

"Liza, when we first came, you were so acceptin' of me, I never felt I had ta really tell you about what brought us here ta begin with."

"Do you want to tell me now, Aidan?"

"Yes, yes I *do*. Well, the man . . . I killed, was part of a group of three who tried ta molest Louisa when I'd run ta hail us a carriage."

"I heard something about that."

"I was around a corner when I heard her scream. I ran ta rescue her and threw one of them aside. Another went ta strike me with his cane, but I hit him first. He was dead before he hit the ground."

"Oh my! But Aidan, I'm not surprised that you did exactly what you did. Still, didn't they consider what the man was doing, and that he tried to strike at you when you . . . were you put on trial?"

"Yes, and sentenced ta servitude. Ye see, the man was a Baron—a low-rankin' nobleman."

"Are they above the law?"

"Apparently so."

"How your life was rocked off course by that one, chance moment!"

"I try not to dwell on it, so's not ta doubt me maker. But at me weakest times, Liza, I still buck against it. The worst part was losin' Louisa, of course. But it's also hard losin' the rights of a free man."

Liza just looked down.

Sensing a trace of resentment, Aidan said, "I'm sorry, Liza. I have no right ta complain ta you about freedom."

After a moment, Liza looked up again and said, "Thank you, Aidan. But my life does make me understand your frustrations better."

"I shouldn't complain. I'm here because of what I did. And it's a better fate than most get for killin' a man. I think back, too, ta the lowest point Jack and I had, just before we met you and the mistress in Washington. I had no idea of the kindness that was waitin' for us here. I just kept tellin' Jackie ta keep believin' that our prayers for goin' to a good place, with good people, were gonna be answered."

"Were they?"

"Of course, Liza, many times over. And you're such a grand part of all that."

"Good. I'm glad. And Aidan, never forget that *someday*, this will end for you and Jack. You won't be servants the rest of your days.

"And there's something else. I truly believe that you and Jack came here for a reason. Look at what having you both here has meant, and done for us. You've made our worship meaningful. We're really learning from the Word, now. And the songs you've helped us create are ministering both to the singers and everyone else."

"Thank you, Liza. I certainly hope that is true."

"Of course it is, not to mention what it means to have you be our friends."

"We feel the same way, Liza, more than I think you know."

"I'm glad, Aidan."

Aidan felt a strong urge to confess his full feelings for Liza, but he was still wary of scaring her away. As he was thinking how to change the subject, he and Liza heard an excited commotion down at the stream.

Liza said, "Sound's like a bite!"

"A big bite!" Aidan agreed.

Then Aidan asked, "Liza, did you like church today?"

"Oh, Ursule's song with the children was wonderful! But I *would* like to know more about the end of the passage you read."

"How do you mean?"

"Well, the way it made a point of saying that all of the plants in God's creation reproduce after their own kind."

"Yes."

"Did you ever wonder whether God is saying that the same is true for people?"

"What is?" called out Mr. Moore, as he and Jack proudly approached with a plump, brown trout.

"Oh, my, Jack! Did you catch him?" Liza asked.

"He sure helped," Mr. Moore insisted, much to Jack's delight.

After the excitement over their catch calmed down, Mr. Moore asked again, "And so what were you saying, daughter, is true for people, too?"

"Oh never mind, Daddy. It was nothing."

"I'm interested, now. Tell your papa."

Liza began uneasily, "I was just wondering if scripture, like Aidan read today, about things reproducing after their own kind isn't saying that the same is true for people."

"In what way, daughter?"

"I suppose . . . for marriage?"

"Well, honey, 'round here, keepin' to one's own kind would be wise if you don't want a whole lot o' folk riled up at ya. But that ain't exactly how the Bible sees it."

"What do you mean, Daddy?"

"Don't want to misspeak, now. But I heard tell Moses had hisself a Ethiopian wife. Seem ta me, ain't but one color a

Ethiopian wife could be. An' that was fine with Moses. After all, he's the one that picked her! But the fact didn't set too well with Moses's sister-in-law, so I recall."

"That would be Aaron's wife," Aidan acknowledged, "Miriam."

"All right, Mr. Aidan, you the preacher. Then you knows the res' of the story."

"No," Aidan said, "but I think I know where to look for it. Maybe I'll read it at church next Sabbath, Mr. Moore. I hope you can join us!"

# Chapter 37

"All right, Chloe girl. Yuh jus' tell Auntie Dee 'zacktly what happened."

"I was restless, Auntie Dee, befo' time come fo' de service dis morning'."

"Mm-hmm."

"Well, I knows I should go ta service, but I starts ta agitate like somethin' don't want me go."

"Da's jus' de devil, gal. Keep talkin'."

"So I figures, I jus' go fo' walk and get time calm down. So I walks down by de springhouse an' pick some wild flower on de way."

"All right."

"Well, Auntie Dee, I ain't never seen de inside o' dis here springhouse. So I decides take a look. I opens up de do' an' steps down in. Every step down, get cooler. Den my eyes starts ta be able see in de dark. I seen all ya got in dere: milk, cream, butter, egg, all in de low trough, an' big melon floatin' in deep hole, where de spring water come up."

"Yes, chile," Auntie said impatiently. "Den what happen?"

"Den, all a-sudden, Snead grab me from behind an' spin me 'round! Auntie, I swear, I don't even know where he come from. All a-sudden he jus' breathin' ol' whiskey breath, right in my face."

"So what he do ta yuh?"

"He keep holdin' me by de shoulders. I tries ta git away, but he too strong. He say, 'What are you doing in here, girl? Come to steal?'

"I say, 'No, jus' ta look.'

"He say, 'If I say you had all those eggs in your apron, then you stole!'"

"What yuh say ta him den?" asked Auntie Dee.

"I too scared. I say nothin'."

"Den what happen?"

"He say, 'You're a fine-lookin' little thing. Best watch your step. I have my eye on you.' Den he look me all up and down, an' smile a smile like ta make my skin crawl. Den he lef'."

"All right, gal. Don't yuh fret. Shouldn't ha' been in de springhouse les' I sends yuh. But yuh didn't do nothin' wrong. Watch where yuh walks all alone. An' nex' Sabbat, git yuhself ta chu'ch!"

"I be dere, Auntie. I promise."

# Chapter 38

As soon as Jack had settled down to sleep after he and Aidan enjoyed their picnic with the Moores, Aidan began to search the scriptures for the account of Moses's Ethiopian wife. He had read the Bible through completely, but did not recall seeing that passage.

But there it was, in the book of Numbers, chapter twelve. The scripture described just what Liza's father had said. Not only did Moses have an Ethiopian wife, but his sister-in-law, Miriam, had objected to her. Soon, though, God dramatically put Miriam in her place.

Aidan couldn't wait to share this passage with the slave family, and with Liza in particular. He drifted off to sleep with those pleasant thoughts on his mind, until he was startled to hear, "Mister Aidan! Mister Aidan!"

He thought he was dreaming until Auntie Dee called out again, "Quick, open up!"

He leapt up, pulled on trousers and opened the door.

"What is it, Auntie?"

"Slabes. We gots muh *runaways!*"

"What?"

Aidan ushered Auntie Dee into the forge.

"Dey come all de way wit' a conductor."

"Is the conductor still here, Auntie?"

"Long gone by now."

"How many are there?"

"Seben."

"Seven!"

"Da's right, Mr. Aidan. Dey's in de kitchen, jus' like befuh."

"I'll be right there," Aidan said, with his head swimming. He checked Jack, and he was sleeping. So Aidan finished dressing and headed for the kitchen.

The new refugees presented a familiar sight. They were dirty, tired, and frightened to death.

"Dis here Mr. Aidan, a good man o' God. He gwan take y'all ta safe place fuh tonight," Auntie Dee assured them.

While she began to put together food and some supplies to sustain the slaves, Aidan tried to calm them.

"We are going ta do all we can ta keep you safe, and get you on your way ta freedom." The word *freedom* brought a look of awe to their faces.

Aidan continued, "You will stay underground while you are here. We'll make you as comfortable as we can. Take care ta be very quiet. In a day or two, someone should come ta take you north."

Then Aidan thought to ask, "Are any of you sick or hurt?"

What happened next tore at his soul. A young girl convinced an old woman to lift her skirt high enough to reveal a gash in her leg that was festering through a filthy bandage. Three other slaves were barefoot, and had various cuts and blisters on their feet. An older man just shook. Aidan couldn't tell whether it was a fever, or just plain fear.

Auntie Dee's common sense took over.

"Mister Aidan, I t'ink we bes' get some wa'm chicken brot' down 'em befuh yuh takes 'em down. An' I still has some biscuits I can heat."

They sat the slaves down while Auntie ministered to this wounded and weary lot. Aidan felt clumsy and awkward, but tried to help the best he could. As tired and afraid as the slaves were, they took such joy in partaking of Auntie Dee's provisions. And they immediately seemed the better for it. What horrors they must have endured to reach this temporary haven of simple comforts. Aidan watched in amazement as Auntie quickly tended to their ailments. Her words and hands soothed them, as they seemed to absorb strength and courage from her.

Sure, now, of how to hide the slaves, Aidan and Auntie Dee decided not to disturb anyone in the big house and risk being overheard. Somehow, Auntie managed to find enough bedding for all.

Less than an hour after they had entered Auntie Dee's kitchen, Aidan began to silently lead the slaves across the lawn of the manse toward the icehouse. Essex, once again, quieted the dogs out in the barn. The moon was bright but, fortunately, there was a spotty cloud cover.

When they reached the icehouse door, though, Aidan faced a problem he hadn't encountered before—how to get the nearly-lame old woman down to the bottom of the pit. He sat her just outside the door, and led the other slaves down the ladder. Then he lit a candle, handed it off to the young girl, and scrambled back up to the door. He beckoned the old woman to him as he stood on the fourth rung down on the ladder. Somehow, he was able to support himself with one arm, and swing her with the other over onto the platform used for lowering slabs of ice.

"You must trust me, now, dearie" he said. "Just stay calm and stay still. You'll be safe, right where you are, if ye hold on to the edge with both hands."

Then Aidan hustled down to the floor and firmly grasped the heavy rope that fed up through the pulleys. He unwound the end of it tied off to a wall anchor and began, ever so slowly, to lower the frightened old woman.

"Ah!" she cried as the platform started to move.

Aidan softly said, "Shush! It's all right," as he prayed, *"Please don't let her fall, Lord!"*

The frayed rope buzzed as it passed through the rumbling pulleys, while the other slaves and Aidan held their breath.

Finally, their precious cargo arrived at a height where they could retrieve her. Then Aidan quietly lowered the platform down the last few feet to the floor.

Ten minutes later, Aidan said goodnight to the runaways in the light of their brightly-burning torches, crawled back through the passageway and reset the timbers. Then he made his way back up to check on his son.

Auntie Dee, who was waiting again with Jack, said she would see Liza first thing in the morning and that Liza, in turn, "gwan hab ta tell de mistress."

Aidan prayed again for the slaves and then tried to drift off to sleep. But a last, disturbing thought invaded his mind. *"How many more will come?"*

As he pondered how they could ever manage more run-aways, he heard a lone hound barking on the property. It kept up long enough that Aidan finally ventured out to the side yard of the manse to try to follow the yelping, which was now being echoed by the dogs in the barn. High on the ridge above the icehouse, Aidan saw the light of a lantern blinking through the woods as its bearer appeared to be pursuing the excited hound. But then the lantern paused, and settled in one spot for several minutes.

Aidan decided to take cover when the light's bearer turned toward him, and began to slowly edge down to a spot on the ridge, just above the icehouse. Then the lantern's flame grew dim, dimmer, and suddenly went out.

# Chapter 39

Auntie Dee went to the manse to see Liza early the next morning.

"Miss Liza!"

"Yes, Auntie Dee, what is it?"

Then Auntie spoke softly. "Slabes, Miss Liza. We gots muh runaways!"

"How many?" Liza asked, with her heart suddenly pounding.

"Seben dem. Come las' night."

"Where are they?"

"Mr. Aidan put 'em down de icehouse cave. We give 'em food an' blankets, fixed up dey bruises. One a ol' woman wit' a gash in 'er leg."

"Oh, Lord, why is this happening?"

"Conductor lef' 'em in de woods again. I don't know if dey t'inks we a safe house, or maybe slave hunters was closin' in on 'em."

"That makes it even worse! If someone finds us out, I can't imagine what they will do to the mistress, let alone to us!"

"I knows, Miss Liza. Mister Aidan say dey has ta stop, too."

"All right, Auntie Dee. Can you get a message to a conductor?"

"Ain't no conductor ta be found. Dis one long gone, an' de las' one takin' cargo up ta Canada."

"But the slaves can't stay here!"

"I knows!"

"All right. I'll tell the mistress."

Liza hated burdening Mrs. Cauley with this new, more complicated problem. The mistress was just getting over the last episode.

"What Liza? How many?" a bewildered Mrs. Cauley asked.

"Seven, including an old woman with a bad leg wound."

"Oh dear, how I wish I could just open my front door and welcome them in. Do they need attending to now?"

"No, Mistress. Auntie Dee and Aidan took care of them and have them down in the icehouse cave."

"All right. For now, that's the best place."

"But there is a complication, ma'am. There's no conductor available to take them on."

"Lord, what are we to do?"

For the next instant, it appeared to Liza as though her mistress was praying with her eyes open.

"I have heard, Liza, that there is a Quaker woman with a safe house nearby."

"Yes, ma'am. She's on the way to Winchester. They say it's a short way on the cutoff road up toward Berryville. Auntie knows which house it is."

"Wouldn't the slaves have a better chance of reaching the North with the Quakers' help?" asked Mrs. Cauley.

"They say many have, Mistress."

"Then we have to get them to the safe house. But seven of them, and not all able to walk! We'll have to use the wagon and—"

"Hide them under something, Mistress."

"Yes, but it can't seem suspicious. Let's see, Essex usually takes the wagon every other week to Winchester for supplies at the big market."

"It's this Friday, Mistress, day after tomorrow."

"Right. So, if we move the slaves into the barn tonight and cover them with straw on the wagon in the morning, Essex can say he's delivering the straw to someone up that way."

"To Master William for his carriage horse?"

"Right, Liza! Essex could deliver the slaves and still make Winchester before dark, if he leaves early enough. He could stay there for the night, go to market early Friday morning and be back to us by supper. It sounds a perfect plan!"

Liza grew quiet.

"What is it, Liza? What unsettles you about this?" asked Mrs. Cauley.

"Ma'am, I believe it may place an awful burden on Essex to do this alone. With more people on the road, making the delivery in daylight is riskier. If he runs into someone asking questions on the way, he could become flustered and draw suspicion."

"I see. Well, all right, I trust your judgment. I will just have to travel with him."

"On the wagon seat?" asked Liza in amazement.

"Yes, of course on the wagon seat. No one will question us then. And remember, I'll appear to just be going to visit overnight at William's."

"Yes, Mistress," Liza nodded. "But you *must* take a parasol and a seat cushion, Ma'am."

"All right, Liza. You are the dearest little mother hen! Now let's pray. Dear Lord, we pray that this hastily fashioned plan did truly originate with thee. Please grant us wisdom, courage, and thy favor as we go. In Jesus's precious name we pray, amen."

# Chapter 40

The next dawn broke before Liza could get a minute's sleep. But as troubled as she was about Mrs. Cauley transporting the runaways, Liza's own weariness and discomfort didn't matter to her. Her only thought, now, was how to best serve her mistress.

"Ms. Isabel, I have your overnight bag packed with the green dress for dinner tonight at Master William's."

"That's fine, Liza."

"Are you ready, then, ma'am?"

"Yes, Liza. Are they prepared for us at the barn?"

"Yes, everything is in ready. Essex and Aidan are waiting for us there. And," Liza whispered, "I have instructions from the Quaker woman."

"What are they?" replied Mrs. Cauley, as she inclined an ear.

"Essex knows which house it is, ma-am. As you approach, look for two white sheets hung on the clothesline off the kitchen. If you don't see them, it is not safe to stop."

"What are we to do then?" puzzled Mrs. Cauley.

"Then your best hope is to continue on to Winchester and hide the slaves there for the night. Someone would have to take them over to the Quaker village at Waterford the next day. Go to the mill and ask for the foreman. Tell him that Holly bid you come. He will take over from there."

"Oh, Liza, this is all starting to sound so complicated, and perilous beyond belief!"

"Mistress, please take courage! If the white sheets are out, all Essex will have to do is pull the wagon around behind the house and into the shed. The Quaker woman is expecting you. We must pray that all will go as planned."

"Oh, you're right, my dear. What would I do without you?"

"Mistress, are you sure you don't want me to go with you?"

"I would cherish your presence, Liza. But I need your eyes, ears, and good sense right here."

Then, in a voice meant to be heard by others, the mistress said, "It's just an overnight trip to visit William and his family. I'll do fine. If they need me to stay, I may tarry another night. Well, then, shall we go?"

Mrs. Cauley and Liza summoned as much courage as they could and made their way out toward the barn. But their hearts sank when they saw Snead rounding the corner to wait for them. They struggled not to panic, but each wondered if Snead had already discovered the cargo of slaves.

"Good morning, Mrs. Cauley. Going somewhare?" he asked, with an accusatory air.

"Yes, Snead. I'm going to check in on my son and his family," Mrs. Cauley replied.

"Why not take the carriage, then? This old wagon bucks and shudders something awful, ma'am."

"I'm deeply touched by your concern, Mr. Snead. But Aidan just repaired the wagon wheels. And William is in need of a load of straw. So we'll make do with a little less comfort, in order to accommodate him."

The mistress and Liza approached the wagon where Aidan and Essex awaited.

"Good morning, Mrs. Cauley," Aidan said.

"Why good morning, Aidan. How is young Jack?"

"He's probably full of Auntie Dee's flapjacks by now, ma'am."

"And all the better for it!" the mistress said, delighted to disengage from Snead.

Aidan helped Mrs. Cauley up onto the wagon seat, and lightly deposited her upon the pillow Essex had provided. Then Liza handed the mistress her open parasol.

"Thank you Liza, and Aidan. It's a fine morning, Essex," the mistress proclaimed.

"Yes, ma'am, fine and blessed."

Snead had been casually examining the load of straw. As Essex took up the reins and prepared for the mistress's command to start off, Snead interrupted.

"Mrs. Cauley, I have a pressing matter I would like to discuss."

A painful silence followed as everyone waited for the mistress to respond.

"It will have to wait until I return tomorrow or the next day, Mr. Snead," she said.

"I'd like for you to think on it during your trip, ma'am."

"What is it, Snead?" replied the mistress impatiently.

"Well, ma'am, things have gotten a bit disheveled over at my abode. I would like to have a maid."

"A *maid*, Snead?"

"Yes, ma'am. I understand young Chloe had been a maid down South, prior. I believe she would do nicely."

"Well, Snead, I think a man being attended, alone, by a young girl would be highly untoward!"

At that, Snead looked back at the load of straw and said, "You know, there might be some who would stop you along the way, ma'am."

"What for, Snead?" snapped the mistress.

"Oh, just seems to me that with *runaways* coming through here, a wagon this size could hold, say, seven slaves hiding under this here loose straw."

Mrs. Cauley looked at Snead with a mixture of terror and growing rage, but said nothing.

He continued, "Well, maybe six healthy ones and one ailing old woman. So why don't you think, Mrs. Cauley, on what I've asked you?"

The mistress turned to look forward again and managed to evenly say, "We can talk when I return, Snead. Essex, *drive on*!"

Snead doffed his cap in mock deference, as the wagon lurched forward. Then he stood with his thumbs hooked around his belt buckle, spit, and said, "I'll look forward to it, Mrs. Cauley, more than you'll ever know."

# Chapter 41

The atmosphere at the next Sabbath's service was one of both joy and fearful concern. To the great relief of those few who had known of their mission, Mrs. Cauley and Essex made it back without incident from delivering the slaves to the safe house. And, this was Aidan's opportunity to present the story of Moses and his Ethiopian wife.

But the threat of Snead knowing the mistress's complicity with the runaways, and his obvious intent to blackmail her into subjecting young Chloe to his crude desires unsettled all those aware of his scheme.

Aidan felt the congregation needed a powerful boost to their spirits. So he began the worship by announcing, "This mornin' we have a special treat in the form of some brand new music! Auntie Dee has been workin' on an upliftin' song that tells what the Lord has done for her."

The little congregation perked up with excitement, and Auntie Dee beamed in anticipation. No one could believe that she'd actually kept her plan to do a song a secret ahead of time.

"But first," Aidan said, "let's open in prayer. Our dear heavenly Father, we come to thee this day in praise of a life transformed by thy love. We also call upon thy might and power to thwart all those who would harm any of thy flock. May our worship, in some way, add to thy great glory. We pray all these things, believin', in the blessed name of our Lord and Savior, Jesus Christ, amen.

"Auntie Dee," cried Aidan, "please come now and tell us all about your song!"

Auntie Dee strode with an air of confidence to stand before them.

"Good mo'nin' y'all on dis bright an' b'utiful Sabbat' day! I jus' start off sayin' dat some y'all *t'inks* yuh knows all 'bout Auntie Dee! An' maybe yuh *does* know 'bout me, pretty much as I iz now. But ain't *nobody* here know'd Auntie Dee be-*fuh* she was walkin' wit' de Lawd.

"Now I weren't no murderuh or robbin' thief, mind. But my eyes wasn't set on all dat's good an' holy, if yuh catch my meanin'."

That statement was greeted by, "Know what you sayin'!"

"'Mos' important t'ing is, I didn't have no joy—no real, 'no matter what happen, Auntie gwan win cause de Lawd *wit'* me,' kind o' joy."

The group encouraged her with calls of, "Un'erstan' dat, Auntie Dee. Go on now, Auntie!"

"Shoot, I weren't gwan tell dis part, but de spirit comin' over me! Well, one day Auntie Dee got married."

There was a communal gasp at this revelation, followed by hoots and hollers.

"Da's right!" Auntie proclaimed. "Got married when I were jus' fifteen. Benjamin de name o' my man. Master down de lowlands didn't take ta no slabes bein' married. Didn't want hab worry 'bout who he splittin' up when he feel like it. But me an' Benjamin done jumped de broom, jus' ta make it legal."

"Praise God! Ya done right!" her friends shouted.

"Well, 'bout a year later, baby boy come along. Name him Isaac cause heard dat name mean 'laughter' in de Bible. An' dat little baby boy come out de womb laughin' ebry time Auntie Dee tickle his belly.

"Den, ober nex' couple year, Auntie lose two babies, probably cause workin' too hard. But me, an' Benjamin, an' Isaac still gets along pretty good. Den one day ol' mastah say he gwan send Benjamin ta work his new plantation up country, place call Aiken where dey commence raisin' horses.

"But mastah say Auntie Dee mus' stay put, so's she can still cook fuh *him!*

"Fuh days, me an' Benjamin talk, cry, moans, an' talks some muh. Finally, Benjamin say he gwan take li'l Isaac wit' him, cause a boy need a daddy. So Auntie Dee start pleadin' ta mastah, 'Don't break up my family!'

"Den mastah say someday he let me go see 'em. But Auntie weren't habin' it. Seen too many 'somedays' dat nebuh comes. So I tells Benjamin, 'Iz bad enough me losin' yuh. Mus' leas'wise leave li'l Isaac wit' me.'

"So in de end, Benjamin let de boy stay. I were so relieft, it almos' make me fuhget losin' my man. I done all I could ta make it up ta de boy fuh not hab no daddy. Took him fishin', throw'd de ball, done all dat.

"Well, one day Auntie all fussin' cause big doin's an' fancy dinner hab make fuh twenty-seben peoples. I cooks from fus' light till company come, jus' befuh suppah. All dat time Isaac were jus' un'erfoot. He keep sayin' he want go fishin' on his own. So I finally lets him. Dat were sometime late in de af'ernoon. An' I know it gwan sound bad, but Auntie Dee so busy, didn't hardly t'ink o' de boy till I sends de las' dessert plate in de dinin' room an' finally sits down. Den Auntie t'ink, *'Oh dear God, where my baby boy!'* Auntie Dee go off a-runnin' down de water, and dere he were, lyin' jus' like asleep. I tries ta wake him, den holds him ta my breas'. Dear Lawd, he seem so cold!

"I picks him up an' runs all de way up de big house, calls from de back do' fuh de mistress come. Weren't no use. Dey foun' on his hand where de snake bit 'um. Say prob'ly was a water moccasent. Dey say Isaac would o' jus' fall asleep wi' de poison. I don't know. I t'ink he suffer. An' fuh long time, Auntie suffer too. Oh, how many time I be sayin', 'How yuh jus' t'inks on yuh wuk, an' not on de boy, yuh only baby boy!'

There was a long pause as all present groaned, cried together and voiced their sympathies.

Then Auntie Dee continued, "I still cries mos' ebry night t'inkin' on dat. But at de time, I cries out ta God, 'Why? Why yuh do dis ta me, Lawd? Yuh takes my man. Den, when Auntie hab muh wuk dan one cook can do, yuh takes my baby! Why? What kinda' God do dis ta Auntie Dee?'

"Well, I didn't 'tend no kind o' wuhship surbice fuh bes' part o' ten year. Eben worse, I done mos' eb'ryt'ing a gal do when she ain't walkin' wi' de Lawd.

"Den one day, I's so miserble, I jus' feels like de prodigal son in dat pig pen. An' dis afta' I done tried ebryt'ing de world say s'posed ta make yuh happy. But nothin' give me joy—jus' muh problems, an' muh problem peoples. I were lower den dat snake's belly.

"So finally, I jus' cries out to de Lawd. Auntie say, 'Lawd, please fuhgib an' cleanse me. Fuhgib me all what I done, an' bad t'ings Auntie Dee say. Didn't mean all dat. Make me clean again, an' give me de new life. Amen.'

"Well, by an' by, de Lawd done all dat an' muh! Ain't got time now tell all de putickaluz. But God work a miracle."

"Hallelujah! Great God Almighty!" the church roared.

"So, dis here my song!" shouted Auntie. "Iz you ready, Mr. Aidan?"

Aidan playfully shouted, "Done *been* ready!" to the delight of all present. He picked up his fiddle and accompanied Auntie Dee as she sang out this heartfelt tune for all she was worth.

## Yuh Pulled Me Up! (Quick Tempo)

I sing my praises to Yuh, Lawd
I jumps right up an' shouts,
Cause Yuh de only one I knows
I really wanna shout about!

Yuh traded me my filt'y rags
Fuh a brand new suit o' joy,
Yuh chased off all my enemies
Now my peace been restored!

CHORUS

Yeah, Yuh pulled me up
Right out o' de pit,
Yuh gave ta me a bran' new life
An' Lawd, dis is it.
Ta love Yuh an' be surbin' Yuh
Ta praise Yuh Holy name,
An' tell de world because o' Yuh
I ain't neber gwan be de same!

Still, sometimes Yuh mus' show me
De backside of Yuh hand,
If da's de only way I'll learn
De t'ings I need ta un'erstan'.

Yuh chastens me wi' mercy, dough
Not like bad mastah do,
If I confess wit' all my heart
Yuh joy come shinin' t'ru!

*CHORUS* — *Yeah, Yuh pulled me up*
*Right out o' de pit,*
*Yuh gave ta me a bran' new life*
*An' Lawd, dis is it.*
*Ta love Yuh an' be surbin' yuh*
*Ta praise Yuh Holy name,*
*An' tell de world because o' Yuh*
*I ain't neber gwan be de same!*

As Auntie Dee shouted out the chorus of her song time and again, she danced with her hands clapping above her head and roused the church to stand and dance right along with her.

She led a procession, in fact, weaving in and out among the log pews. Then she had everyone make a circle around the pews to form a "shout ring." Auntie Dee played song leader, singing out just a few words or a line, and having the others repeat as her chorus.

Aidan was amazed at the many variations of melody the shout produced. Everyone took part in adding a new twist, and different harmonies as well. It all flowed out so naturally, with perfect pitch and rhythm. Jack was delighted and enjoyed the shout as much as anyone, as he felt every beat of the music!

Finally, fully winded and joyous in the Lord, Auntie and all present exclaimed a resounding "Amen!"

Then the congregation laughed and cried at Auntie's story, moaned, and praised Jesus. Everyone hugged Auntie Dee, told her they loved her and meant it.

Finally, Aidan asked, "Would anyone still like to hear a bit of the Word?"

They did, so he began, "I am pleased that Mr. Walter Moore has joined us again this mornin'. Mr. Moore told me recently about a passage of scripture that I never recalled readin'. It is an interestin' one, because I believe it has much ta tell us about how God sees the different races of people he created."

"Dat right? Come on now, preach it!"

"Now Moses, of course, was a Jew. Generally speakin', Jews in the Bible were what we would consider ta be a white race. And Moses would be among them. But there is a very interestin' description of a wife Moses had taken in the book of Numbers, chapter twelve. It turns out that she was *not* of the white race."

At this, the slaves were amazed!

"No, she was an *Ethiopian* woman—an African. And there were some close to Moses who did not accept her because of that. Moses's brother, Aaron, and his wife, Miriam, were critical of Moses's Ethiopian wife. But listen to this passage and see what the Lord thought of their ill feelings toward the woman."

Aidan read in a stark, dramatic tone:

"And the anger of the Lord was kindled against them; and he departed.

"And the cloud departed from off the tabernacle; and, behold, Miriam became leprous, white as snow: and Aaron looked upon Miriam, and, behold, she was leprous.

"And Aaron said unto Moses, 'Alas, my lord, I beseech thee, lay not the sin upon us, wherein we have done foolishly, and wherein we have sinned.

"'Let her not be as one dead, of whom the flesh is half consumed when he cometh out of his mother's womb.'

"And Moses cried unto the Lord, saying, 'Heal her now, O God, I beseech thee.'

"And the Lord said unto Moses, 'If her father had but spit in her face, should she not be ashamed seven days? Let her be shut out from the camp seven days, and after that let her be received in again.'

"And Miriam was shut out from the camp seven days: and the people journeyed not till Miriam was brought in again."

Then Aidan asked, "What does this tell us about how God feels about those who judge based on the color of someone's skin?"

Auntie Dee said, "I think it show God don't like none o' dat, not one bit."

"Yes. And who seems more at fault in this sin, Moses's brother, Aaron, or his wife, Miriam?" Aidan asked.

Henderson raised his hand.

"Yes, Henderson."

"Well, I would say Miriam, because I figure she were de one dat start all de talkin'."

Auntie chimed in quickly, "Why you say dat, jus' cause she a *woman?*"

Henderson calmly replied, "Nothin' ta do with it. I reckon it must o' been her dat started it, cause de Lawd strike *her* down wi' leprosy. In fact, seem like He sayin' ta her, 'All right, gal, you think you better jus' cause you white? I'll make you even whiter, wit' de leprosy. See how you mighty self like dat!'"

Chuckling a bit, Aidan said, "That's a good observation, Henderson. But Aaron seems ta be admittin' some guilt, too, when he says, 'wherein *we* have sinned.' So could it be that even if we just *go along* with someone who is wrongly judgin' another person, in the Lord's eyes, we have ta share the guilt?"

"Reckon so, prob'ly right," the congregation agreed.

"And there is somethin' else we can see about how God thinks in this story," Aidan continued. "It is interestin' ta see that the Ethiopian woman was not Moses's servant. She was his *wife*."

"Tha's right!"

"And, after all, Moses was no ordinary man. What proof do we have that God viewed him in a special way? Yes, Fanny."

"Well Mr. Aidan, everbody know how God picked Moses ta lead de Chillun o' Israel out de wilderness."

"That's right, Fanny. And, a little earlier in the passage, it is even written that Moses was the only man God spoke directly to, and not through a prophet. So let me ask, is there any sign in these scriptures that God objected to Moses being married to a woman of color?"

Aidan listened with great interest as Liza began to speak.

"Well, of course not. Just the opposite. God was very irritated when someone tried to say that the Ethiopian woman was not good enough for Moses."

"So what does this tell us about how God views the races?" Aidan asked.

Jupiter spoke up. "I reckon it say dat God jus' figure, we all de same."

This was met with unanimous agreement.

"I believe that is right," Aidan said, "because we are all made in *his image.* So, we are *all* precious in his sight. Would someone like to close us with prayer?"

After a pause when no one offered, Liza volunteered. "Dear Lord, thank you for your marvelous Word. Thank you for the way it reaches out to us over thousands of years, and tells us who you are and who *we* can *be*. We love you, Lord. Please bless us through this reading."

And all present said, "Amen!"

# Chapter 42

"Ms. Isabel!" Liza proclaimed in a nervous whisper as she reached the top of the stairs and scurried across the hallway into Mrs. Cauley's bedchamber.

"Yes, what it is, Liza?" replied the mistress.

"Mr. Snead is in the front parlor. He said he wants to speak with you."

Clearly irritated, Mrs. Cauley said, "I know what he wants. Just let him wait. I'll go down directly."

Snead was about to underestimate the mistress again. While in Winchester, Mrs. Cauley had telegraphed her husband because of Snead's request. Without going into detail, she'd let her husband know that an emergency had arisen that required his presence. Mr. Cauley responded that he was leaving immediately and that, by riding late into the evenings, he would arrive the following day.

Even though the mistress was increasingly worried about how her husband would react to all that had transpired, she had no doubt that he would refuse to agree to Snead's horrible demand.

As she reached the foot of the staircase, Mrs. Cauley was incensed at the sight of Snead's unsavory presence in her front parlor. As she entered, she remained standing to make the exchange as brief as possible.

"Yes, Mr. Snead. What is it?"

"I believe you know what I'm here about, ma'am. I want to know whether you are going to provide me Chloe as my maid."

"I told you previously, Mr. Snead, that I thought the idea to be objectionable in the extreme. But my husband will be arriving here tomorrow. He shall address the situation with you at his convenience."

"I'm glad of it, Mrs. Cauley. But if you were to convince him, yourself, that this is a right idea, I would not have to use any further means of persuasion, if you catch my meaning."

"You may attempt to use whatever means you dare, Mr. Snead. But you would be wise to know that my husband is not a man to be trifled with. Good day."

"And a good day to you, Mrs. Cauley."

Despite her resolute front, the mistress thanked God that Liza was there for her to confide in. Liza asked, "What will you do, ma'am? Will you tell Master Cauley everything that has happened?"

"I must, Liza. Before Snead asserted himself, I prayed that it would be all right to just let our episodes with the runaways pass and be forgotten. I have no choice, now, but to be fully forthcoming with Mr. Cauley. He is a good, and most decent man. I know he'll be deeply troubled by what occurred. But I trust my love will not side against me in the end."

Mrs. Cauley had slept very little when she heard the whinny of her husband's steed as he galloped in the lane the next day. She descended the stairs quickly to receive Mr. Cauley in the front parlor.

"My darling!" the master shouted, as he ran in to embrace her.

"Dearest William!" she returned, as she fought back tears.

"What is it, Isabel? What has vexed you so to summon me?

"It is a situation that has arisen involving Snead."

"Has he been out of line?"

"In a manner."

"I'll go set him straight right now!"

"No, William!" she protested. "Please, just let's sit and discuss this *calmly* after you've refreshed yourself from your journey."

"All right, but if he has taken liberties!"

"No. But he has made a request for himself. I'm stopping at that for now. Please, just take a moment to relax and I'll arrange some refreshment for you."

Mrs. Cauley had rehearsed her conversation with her husband for days on end. But now, faced with the situation firsthand, she was truly at a loss where to start. She nervously prayed for guidance.

Returning shortly with a tray she said, "Here you are, my dear. Auntie has prepared a light snack."

"I can't eat with this suspense, but I am thirsty!" the master proclaimed, as he gulped a glass of cider. Wiping his lips, he said, "Now, Isabel, tell me *all* that's happened."

Mrs. Cauley went to close the door behind her to create privacy. The master quickly followed her lead by shutting the other door to the room. When his wife took a seat on a large settee, Mr. Cauley came and sat beside her.

Then the mistress began quietly, "Right after you departed for Richmond, William, we had an enormous surprise. Runaway slaves arrived here who had heard that the new slaves who recently came from your uncle's estate, had come here to a better way of life."

"Dear Lord, Isabel, what did you do with them?"

"I realized the seriousness of our complicity in harboring them, and relied upon our most trusted servants to arrange for the runaways to leave the next day."

"Leave? Where to?"

"Well, with a guide who would take them north to—"

"You helped runaway slaves escape on the *underground railroad*?"

"William! What else could I have done?"

"You could have held them for return to their rightful owner!"

"But you didn't *see* them, and hear their desperation. And, after all, they came here because—"

"Because what?"

"They came here because we are *good* to our *servants*! How could I not be good to *them*?"

Mr. Cauley leaped up and began to pace. The mistress had never seen him so agitated! Back and forth he strode, turning and pacing, turning and then nearly *lunging* at her as he choked out the words, "Why didn't you let *me* deal with this?"

"There was no time!" she pleaded, as she started to quiver. Then she cried, "William, you're *frightening* me!"

Mr. Cauley shuddered himself, but then slowly sat down and stared away from his wife as he struggled to compose himself and control his rage within. But his mind raced frantically with the thoughts, "*We're ruined! Our son's ruined! I'll lose my assembly seat. We may lose our land. I could go on trial! No friend will acknowledge us. How could she be so stupid? How could she be so naive?"*

He jumped up again and strode quickly to a window to look out on the familiar scene of the place he loved and always longed to return to. Would he lose it all now? Would he lose everything that was dear to him, because of *this*?

He turned and looked at his wife's fearful trembling. He began to recognize her agony at what she was putting him through. Then, without changing his grim expression, he came again to sit beside her.

Very solemnly, Mrs. Cauley continued, "The opportunity to move them along came so quickly. And I have no idea the particulars of how Auntie Dee arranged for their flight. But when that resolution sprang up, I had to seize upon it."

"Who else knows about this?" Mr. Cauley said.

"Auntie, of course, Liza, Essex and Aidan."

"Not Snead?"

"Well, he didn't know about the first group."

"The *first* group! There have been more?"

Sobbing again, Mrs. Cauley hesitated at telling him more. But with resignation, she finally admitted, "Yes! Within days a second group that included an old woman with a serious leg wound appeared at night. We tried to handle them the same way as the first, all the while praying that God would prevent more from following."

"Go on," her husband said, as he closed his eyes and let his chin sink to his chest.

"We hid them in a little cave just off the icehouse pit."

"Yes, I'm aware of it. What happened next?"

"Well, somehow Snead observed the second group."

"Did he say as much?"

"He implied knowledge when we had them hidden in the hay wagon, and were about to take them to a Quaker safe house on the cutoff road to Berryville. Snead confronted me as Essex and I were about to leave under the ruse of visiting our William with a load of straw for his stable."

Mr. Cauley turned to look at his wife and asked, "Why could they not be escorted on the underground as the others had?"

"All the conductors were in Canada."

"Well, I must give you credit for ingenuity, Isabel . . . and courage."

With a hint of tenderness, Mr. Cauley said, "Go on."

"Snead appeared just as we were about to depart, and nearly demanded that our young girl, Chloe, be given to him as his personal maid."

"That is *outrageous!*"

"Of course. But when I put him off, he coyly remarked that the load of straw we were transporting might be construed as a hiding place for the exact number of slaves we had hidden, including an old woman."

"That is blackmail!"

"Indeed! But my dear William," the mistress implored as she extended her arms to embrace him, "what, in God's name, are we to do now?"

# Chapter 43

Although Chloe had served well as a general household maid in Mississippi, Liza was chosen to train her in the ways of serving at High Meadows. In the midst of all the turmoil Snead was causing, Liza decided to cut the tension by involving Chloe in a meaningful diversion.

"Chloe, have you given any more thought to working on your song with Mr. Aidan?"

"I ain't sure, Miss Liza."

"But after you saw what it did for Auntie Dee when she sang her song, you said you wanted to have one, too, right?"

"Yes. But I have embarrassment."

"Why, Chloe? None of the things you told me about were your fault."

"Maybe it because Mr. Aidan is a man."

"But a very understanding man. I can take you to him, if you like."

Chloe squirmed a bit. But then she looked up at Liza's unwavering, hopeful expression.

"OK, Miss Liza. I go."

"Fine. Our usual work is finished for now, and the mistress is having her reading time. I'll ask her if we can walk over to the forge. We'll go see if Mr. Aidan can make time for us."

As they walked along, Chloe said, "Miss Liza, I got a question befo' we gets dere."

"What is it, Chloe?"

"What if my song no good?"

"That's not very likely. I've heard Mr. Aidan say that if you have passion for what your song is about, it will come through in the words you choose and in the singing. And I know you feel passion about what happened to you, Chloe."

"I do, Miss Liza."

As they approached the forge, Liza was reassured by the steady sound of hammer meeting iron.

"Hello, Mr. Aidan!" she called above the noise. "Is this a good time to bring a new songwriter to speak with you?"

Aidan turned to see Chloe with Liza, wiped his hand on his "clean" rag, then shook hands gently with Chloe and said,

"Thank you for comin', Chloe. Hello, Liza. Please, let me find you both a seat."

Aidan removed a saddle from a stool, and positioned two chairs with it in a little circle. Then Jack popped in from the sleeping room and ran to give Liza a hug.

Everyone visited for a moment, then Aidan asked Jack, "Son, could you excuse yourself for just a bit so I can speak with Chloe about something we need to talk about?"

After a mild protest, Jack slumped off to his quarters but turned and gave Liza a wink before closing the door.

Then Aidan said, "Chloe, I feel so good that you trust me enough ta talk about your song."

"Well, I'm gwan try, Mr. Aidan. But I ain't bold like my brother, Brister."

"I see Brister about. Do you know why he doesn't join us for services?" Aidan asked.

Looking suddenly at the floor, Chloe said, "I can't tell you dat to your face, Mr. Aidan."

"Is it because I am white, and I lead part of the service?" he asked softly.

"You readin' my mind, Mr. Aidan."

"It's all right, Chloe. I hope, in time, Brister will come ta trust me, too. Can I ask you a question?"

"Yes, sir."

"What made you want to write a song?"

"Well, I seen what it done fo' everbody who already done it. When Auntie Dee sung her song, I know'd fo' sure, cause it make her an' everbody else feel so good."

"OK, good. But let's just pretend now, alright? How do you think people will feel after they hear *your* song?"

"If dey has any feelin's at all, dey gwan feel real sad."

"That's fine, Chloe. Because a song like yours will have power, the power to help make things better. Someday it may even keep someone from doin' to another woman or girl what I think happened to you. That makes you bein' brave enough ta make the song really worth it."

Encouraged by his comments, Chloe said a bit more forcefully, "Den, Mr. Aidan, dis gwan be a song 'bout how my heart got broke."

Aidan drew Chloe out as gently as he could about being brutally raped, and later having her beloved child torn away from her because of a jealous mistress. Liza moved to Chloe's side and held her, as her story came out in starts and stops. Parts overlapped, or sprung out of order. But Aidan listened intently to every word.

Then he asked, "Chloe, have you ever just sat and thought all the way through the hard things that happened to you, start to finish?"

"Yes, Mr. Aidan," Chloe said, as she warmed to the thought. "An' I can tell you right where. Down Mississippi, when de work done, I go sits by de river. Some reason, watchin' dat water flow on by kinda' he'p me ta think. So, durin' all d'ose times, I jus' be sittin' at de river's edge, a little life on my mind."

"That's it!" Aidan exclaimed.

"Da's what, Mr. Aidan?"

"Chloe, that's the beautiful beginnin' ta your song!"

# Chapter 44

"Good morning, Brister," Liza said, as she encountered Chloe's brother on the path to the slave quarter.

"Mornin', Miss Liza," he returned warily.

"Brister, I'm glad to see you. I'd like to talk about something."

"Whatever it is, I didn't do it."

Liza said good-naturedly, "Sounds like you're used to being blamed for things!"

"Happen all de time, 'specially when I'm jus' mindin' my own business."

"Ah, I usually mind my own business, too," she replied, "unless I know that I can be of help. Brister, I want you to do me a special favor."

"Wha's that?" he asked with his head turned to the side.

"I want you, just this once, to come try our Sunday service. If you don't like it, no need to come again."

"That blacksmith gwan preach y'all?"

"Yes, and we're very lucky to have him."

"Then I won't be there."

"But why, Brister?"

"Miss Liza, you a real nice lady. An' these here Cauley people mus' treat you real good. I give 'em that. But it weren't like that fo' us down South.

"I seen my sister *raped* by a white man. I been beat, many time, by white mens. They think we's jus' dogs. Six days a week, I labor. And I labors good enough. But Sunday de one day tha's all mine. Las' thing I'm gwan do is sit there an' have some white man tell me how I's s'posed ta live."

"But Mr. Aidan isn't like—"

"He de one havin' y'all make up them songs, right?"

"Right. It's a meaningful part of our service."

"Well, I been makin' up my own song. An' you know what?"

Trying not to lose her patience, Liza replied, "What, Brister?"

"I didn't need no white man ta help me make it!"

Liza surprised Brister, then, by asking, "Fine. Why don't you sing it for me?"

Brister backed up a couple of paces and made an effort to compose himself. Then he hummed the opening lines, as he kept the beat by slapping a hand on his leg. Thus rehearsed, he cleared his throat and began in earnest.

*Kain't No White Man Tell Me (Mid Tempo)*

*I seen me de white man*
*Some short an' some tall,*
*Ta me they's de same*
*Two bob, tha's all.*

*Be callin' me niggah*
*Like they callin' a dog,*
*Come Sunday start preachin'*
*How I needs de Lawd.*

*CHORUS*

*Kain't no white man tell me*
*Wa's wrong an' wa's right,*
*Them devils don't walk*
*In no Holy light.*
*I won't believe whippin'*
*Is what I deserve,*
*An' my sistah hate*
*What they forcin' on her.*

House niggahs be sayin'
My heart grow too mean,
They works for white folk
Jus' nice as can be.

Them niggahs ain't workin'
No hot dusty fields,
Take my blood an' sweat
Jus' makin' `em yield.

CHORUS

Kain't no white man tell me
Wa's wrong an' wa's right,
Them devils don't walk
In no Holy light.
I won't believe whippin'
Is what I deserve,
An' my sistah hate
What they forcin' on her.

# Chapter 45

Jack was moved by Auntie Dee's song at the church service, and he was deeply troubled by Auntie losing her son.

After watching Jack mope around all day, Aidan said, "Why don't you go pay Auntie Dee a visit after supper? Take her somethin' special ta show her that you care, and tell her how sorry you are that she lost her boy. You'll feel better, Jack. And I imagine Auntie Dee will, too."

When Jack arrived at the kitchen, Julia was just finishing scrubbing the last pot. Auntie Dee took one look at Jack and her face lit up. She knew this was a special visit because, as she later recalled, "He were all shined up like a new penny. Eben hab his hair combed!"

Auntie Dee said, "Lookie here, Julia. It's my Jackie boy!"

"Hey, Master Jack," said Julia.

"Hey, Julia," Jack replied, adopting her style of greeting.

Julia spied what Jack held behind his back and figured it best to leave Auntie Dee and her young admirer alone.

"Auntie Dee," Julia said. "All de pots is put up. Thought I'd go on down de quarter, see Ursule."

Auntie Dee smiled and waved for her to go. Then Auntie proclaimed, "Yuh come jus' de right time, Jackie. Work all done an' time fuh li'l wizit."

"I picked these special for you, Auntie Dee!" Jack said, as he proudly handed her a bunch of pretty wild flowers.

"Oh my!" Auntie exclaimed, as she held the flowers up to her breast. "Dese fuh me? I ain't had a gen'leman give me flower in many a day. An' how pretty! T'ank yuh, dear Jackie boy!"

Auntie quickly found a pretty glass bottle to put them in, added some water, and placed the flowers on the table in front of them.

"Dere," she said. "Now everbody come in Auntie's kitchen can see 'em. Dis such a nice t'ing yuh done. An', let me see," she said playfully. "Did I bake anyt'ing dat a young boy would like taste of?"

Jack began licking his lips as Auntie Dee undertook her usual faux search through various food jars for about as long as Jack could stand it. Finally, she exclaimed, "Lookie here! Foun' a whole batch o' fresh cinnamon cookies!"

She and Jack got settled, he with his cookies and milk, Auntie with her sassafras tea.

Then she asked, "Now, young man, what on yuh mind?"

"Well, Auntie Dee, I really did want to see you."

"Well, I'm glad o' dat!"

"But I wanted to *tell* you something, too."

"I thought so. What de sumpin'?"

"I was feeling bad, Auntie."

"'Bout what?"

"Well, because of when you sang your song at the church meeting."

Auntie teased, "What, yuh don't like my singin'?"

Jack started to giggle and said, "No, Auntie Dee. You sing the best!"

"What make yuh sad, den?"

"It's what you said *before* you sang your song."

"Mm-hmm. When I talk about my boy," she said softly.

"Yes, when you told how he was killed when the snake bit him."

"Um, dat were a very sad time. I loved dat boy so much."

"I know how you feel because . . ." but Jack couldn't finish.

"Cause yuh loved yuh Momma dat much, too," Auntie said tenderly.

Jack's face started to brighten. "How did you know what I was going to say?"

"Cause we t'inks so much alike, Jackie an' Auntie Dee. Da's sumpin' special we got, you an' me."

"Then did you ask God the same thing I did?"

"Mm-hmm," Auntie said. "I ast him, dear Lawd, if yuh loves Auntie Dee so much, how come yuh takes away somebody *I* loves so much?"

"That's what I asked him, too!"

"See, tol' yuh."

"Well?"

"Well what?"

"Well, did God give you an answer, Auntie Dee?"

"Yep, but took awhile."

"Why does God take such a long while?"

"Because dat teach us patience. An' patience build our fait'. Udderwise, if God jus' gib us all we wants, right when we wants it, den we don't hab ta wait an' learn ta trus' him fuh nothin' in de fus' place."

"So then, Auntie Dee, after it took a long while, what did God end up telling you?"

"He tol' me dat if I trusts him, I will know de why an' de the how of it all, by an' by. Now, dis here de important part. He promise if I *really* trusts him, he will meet my ebry need."

"So how did he meet your need?"

"Yuh silly t'ing!" she said, tickling Jack's belly. "He done brought me *you*!"

After more giggles, asking for another cookie and making a little milk burp, Jack finally said, "Well, I think we're the same again about something else."

"Wha's dat?"

"I think maybe God, like the way he brought you another boy to love? Well, I think he brought me a new momma to love."

"Dat so? Is dis here new momma someone Auntie Dee know?"

Jack got all giggly and said, "Guess!"

"Le's see," said Auntie thoughtfully. "Can't be Ms. Isabel, cause she already married."

"No!"

"Maybe it Julia. She a good worker."

"No!"

"No? Well, can't be me cause Auntie too old and fat."

"I don't think you're that old."

Auntie grabbed Jack and tickled him again.

"An' what about de fat part?"

"Oh, Auntie, I love you just like you are!"

"Listen ta dis li'l politician," Auntie said. "Lawd, what I has ta put up wit'. OK, one more guess. Miss Liza."

"Hallelujah!"

"Hallelujah? Now yuh soundin' jus' like *me*!"

"It's her! It's Miss Liza. I mean, I hope so."

"You know what, Jackie boy?"

"What?"

"Auntie hope so too," she said, as she drew Jack to her, kissed the top of is head and rocked him in her warm embrace.

# Chapter 46

Once again, Mrs. Cauley was restless. The weight of her battle against Snead and the uncertainty of what would happen if he informed against her, kept the mistress of High Meadows agitated and miserably awake.

And though she was thrilled to share her bed once more with her beloved husband, Mrs. Cauley mourned his tossing and turning, caused by the same concerns.

Somewhere in the moments just before dawn, she suddenly realized that Mr. Cauley no longer lay beside her. She arose, donned a robe and slippers, and found him dressed and seated in the dining room before a roughly assembled breakfast.

"My dear," she said, stifling a yawn, "what are you about so early this morning?"

"I've formed a plan my darling, or providence did, about an hour ago. It involves my brother, Stephen."

"Shh," Mrs. Cauley gently cautioned. She checked to make sure that no one was about who could overhear them. Then she quietly asked, "Stephen? How can he aid us?"

"Do you recall me telling you of Stephen's standing offer?"

"To come join in his law practice in Washington City?"

"Yes, my dear. He has been quite insistent upon it. And that city is bustling with all manner of commerce related to the federal government."

"But William," she said, trying to steady herself as she took a seat, "it is one thing for your younger brother to leave your family's holdings. But as firstborn, you are far too much a son of this valley to think of leaving High Meadows. This is your true home. Surely, this place runs too strongly in your blood to ever wish to leave it!"

"My dear, I have no desire to unduly alarm you, but you must understand. There are laws being formed in several legislatures that would change our lives forever should you–should *we* be found guilty of harboring and aiding runaways. And you mean more to me than any farmland or old homestead."

Mrs. Cauley grasped one of her husband's hands with both of hers and squeezed it tightly.

Then Mr. Cauley continued, "Isabel, Washington is our best chance. And it will take the utmost secrecy to ensure our flight."

"But what can we take with us under these circumstances?" Mrs. Cauley asked. "What about our servants? And who will occupy our home and land?"

"Those are details to be determined, my dear. I know that Robert Anthony is sure to have legal insight concerning our holdings. I can appoint him as trustee of our estate until we become settled. But for now, I must ride at first light to Winchester to telegraph Stephen and await his reply. In the interim, I will attempt to speak with Robert. If Stephen bids us come, we must leave almost immediately."

"But surely, William, you'll need a manservant. And I need Liza. She is my right arm. And I can't imagine our lives without Auntie. And, oh dear, there is a new development. Liza cannot be asked to leave without Aidan and his son."

"Why, my dear?"

"Liza and Aidan are in love."

"Dear God!" the master exclaimed. "What *else*?"

"It would be savage to leave young Chloe behind, too, for obvious reasons."

"All right, then. They can all become part of our new household. When I am able, I will make inquiry on Aidan's behalf regarding work in Washington for a blacksmith. I have no time to retrieve Isaac, whom I left in my haste, in Richmond. I can train Essex to assist me, and he can drive you in the carriage. We'll send for Isaac, later.

"Prepare to leave as cautiously as you can, without raising suspicions. Whomever you must call into confidence, simply tell them to trust you, and to say nothing of this to another soul."

"Of course," replied Mrs. Cauley. "I'll only need to confide in Liza for now. But what if Snead should ask again?"

"Tell him I was called to Winchester on business, but that I will speak with him tomorrow."

Gazing outside, Mr. Cauley said, "I can see a trace of light now, Isabel, coming through the trees. I must go. Take my hand, my love. Let's commit our plans to the Lord. Dear gracious heavenly Father, we thank and trust thee that these forming plans have come from thy great wisdom and insight. We lay them before thee, beseeching thy blessing upon them. Oh, grant us thy speed, discernment, and grace. In the blessed name of Jesus Christ our Lord we pray, amen."

"Oh William, hold me."

Mr. Cauley embraced his wife and, for the moment, let his strength dispel her most pressing doubts and fears.

# Chapter 47

Throughout Liza's time of service, she had never seen her mistress in such a grave, determined state. At first, she wondered whether Snead had already informed authorities of Mrs. Cauley's aid to the runaways.

"Dear Liza, I trust you slept well, because we are about to work like we've never worked before."

"Yes, Mistress," Liza assured her. "I did sleep fairly well."

Mrs. Cauley closed her bedchamber door and led Liza to a far corner of the room. "Excellent, Liza, because we have much to accomplish today. We are going to prepare for a change, an important change. It will require that we trust in the Almighty, in Mr. Cauley and I dare say, in each other to the utmost. Will you commit to that Liza?"

"Of course, mistress. I trust you, the Lord, and the master with my life."

As Liza answered her, Mrs. Cauley searched her maid's face for any sign of reticence.

"I'm so relieved at your answer, Liza. Now I shall take you into my deepest confidence. Mr. Cauley has charted a plan to foil Snead's plot to ruin us. We are about to leave High Meadows."

"Leave, Mistress?" Liza blurted out. She quickly covered her lips, then whispered, "Leave High Meadows?"

"Yes, my dear. And when I said 'we,' that included you. I cannot imagine managing without you."

"Thank you, Mistress. But will you—"

"Take others? Yes. Aidan, Jack, Auntie, Essex, and Chloe. Isaac will join us later."

At this, Liza was somewhat relieved. But the shock of the mistress's news was still causing her to feel faint. She immediately thought of her father, and whether she would ever see him again.

"Where, Ms. Isabel? Where are we to *go*?"

"North, to Washington City. We will live somewhere near Mr. Cauley's brother, Stephen. He has an excellent law practice, and is well-connected in the federal government. The master will join his firm there."

"I can't even imagine it, Mistress. But if you bid me go, of course I will."

Mrs. Cauley held Liza's hands for a moment and said, "That's what I prayed you would say. I am as apprehensive as you, Liza. But together, with God's help, we can do this. I know not whether this shall be a permanent arrangement, or only last for a time. But regardless, we shall make it possible for you to see your father again."

"Oh thank you, Mistress."

"Of course. Now, we must set about selecting bare necessities that will carry us through our journey, and the first weeks after our arrival in Washington."

"Yes, ma'am."

"Liza, if we work on my things first, I'm sure that will help you make your own selections later. But know that we must finish *today*."

"What if someone notices I am not attending my regular duties, Mistress?"

"Tell anyone who questions you that we are taking a day for organizing. Say that you'll return to regular duties tomorrow."

"Yes, ma-am. And Mistress, thank you."

"For what, dear?"

"Thank you for Aidan and Jack."

Mrs. Cauley hugged Liza like a mother.

# Chapter 48

In her whirlwind of intense activity, it seemed to Mrs. Cauley as though her husband had been gone for days. Remarkably, he returned from a very successful trip to Winchester by suppertime that same evening.

"Dear William," she exclaimed, as he bounded into their bedchamber, "how did thee fare today?"

"I am having difficulty believing all that transpired, Isabel! But one door after another opened so completely that, by day's end, a clear plan had been affirmed in my mind many times over."

"That is so encouraging! I shall have dinner served here in our chambers so you can share all with me in confidence. Please lie down and rest for awhile, as I arrange for the meal."

William's news was exactly what Mrs. Cauley needed to hear. He was confident now, not perplexed and searching as he had been so early that morning. And his confidence was beginning to give the mistress hope of the rightness of his plan.

As she was about to depart their chamber for the kitchen, Mr. Cauley startled from his repose and said, "My dear, would you get word to Liza, Aidan, young Jack, Essex, and Chloe to quietly go out to the kitchen at, say, eight this evening? We shall speak to them there with Auntie Dee. You and I will appear to be stopping by to show appreciation to Auntie for an especially good meal."

"Yes, William, of course."

As the mistress went about discreetly making those arrangements, her spirit led her to pray one thing above all others. "*Lord, please prevent Snead from suspecting anything as we make our way through these next crucial hours. Grant us wisdom and strength. In Jesus's name.*"

Liza offered to inform all parties required to meet out in the kitchen, and swore them to secrecy. Essex and Chloe had to be assured that they had done nothing wrong.

Mrs. Cauley returned to the bedchamber and lay beside William for a few precious moments of rest. She thought, "*How many times have I stared at this ceiling beneath which I've shared affection, borne children, lay in sickness, planned countless days, laughed, cried, worried, and prayed about it all?*"

Then her mind returned to the packing she and Liza had done. It occurred to her during the course of the day that, in addition to including basic necessities, she would need to take important possessions that could never be replaced. She packed the family Bible, tintypes and small likenesses of family, precious letters, and all of Mr. Cauley's legal documents and bank instruments which he had carefully gathered and shown her in case of ill fortune during his travels.

Then she focused on other keepsakes and valuable jewelry. There was no room for artwork and most of the silver service, despite the considerable value they held. And to remove them would have raised suspicions among the household staff. She did hope to have select items sent along to them, once they were settled.

The remainder of their day was spent deciding what to take from both the master's and Mrs. Cauley's clothing, her toilet articles and their bedding. Then they sorted through Liza's things. In effect, they had faced the formidable task of making decisions, in one day, that could easily have occupied a week or more in a normal course of events.

The process was not only taxing in its demand to make right choices. It also made the mistress and Liza fight back tears as countless family memories flowed from the items that came to hand. Still, the gravity of the situation had pushed them onward.

Now Mrs. Cauley wrestled with the thought, "*Why can't we just eliminate this wretched, Phineas Snead by some apparent accident or anonymous attack? Isn't he widely reviled? Couldn't any number of people have wished to see him get his due?*"

Soon enough, though, she begged forgiveness for that thought. But that didn't prevent her from pointedly asking Mr. Cauley as soon as he awoke, "Sweetheart?"

"Yes, my dear," he replied with a yawn.

"Might I ask, could we not simply *pay* Snead to leave our lives forever?"

"No, Isabel, not in the sense of hush money," Mr. Cauley replied.

"But why? A devil such as he surely has his price."

"Any payment we would make to Snead to keep him quiet would simply be the first in his unending demands upon us. Our secret will make us just as vulnerable to him if revealed in a month or two, as it does today."

She patted her husband's chest and agreed, "You are right, William, I know it."

"Don't dismay, Isabel. As I said, we now have a plan," Mr. Cauley assured.

The mistress could hear Julia's footfall on the stairs as she carried their meal to them. Mrs. Cauley quickly arose and cleared space on a table. Then she and her husband sat down to a lovely final meal at High Meadows.

Soon Mr. Cauley said in a low tone, "Let me tell you now, Isabel, of our planned course of action. Robert and William helped to chart it."

"You saw our son today, too?"

"Yes, right after my visit with Robert. I actually found Robert at the inn. I'd sent my telegram to Stephen, and he replied almost immediately. He is overjoyed! He said that he is quite put upon with the demands of a new project, and sees our desire to come as a clear answer to his prayers. He wants me to assist him with an important procurement contract immediately."

"Wonderful! So you discovered Robert at the inn?"

"Yes, Isabel. Robert's clerk told me he was dining with a client. As I arrived, they were just finishing up."

"You didn't have to wait for him, then. Providence! Did you take time to eat?"

"Indeed. And as I did, Robert had time to ponder what I quietly told him of our situation. He has such a keen, ordered mind. He quickly agreed that it is wise to move on to Washington City, for a time."

"For a time?" said the mistress, with rising hope. "Does that mean there is a chance of our return?"

"Eventually, my dear. But much depends on how Snead responds to his severance offer."

"What does that mean, precisely?"

"Well, back to the plan. We will secret away tonight just after midnight, and it will be rightly claimed that I was summoned on urgent government business to live and work in Washington City."

"All right."

"Robert, as my legal representative, will arrive here at first light with William."

"William?"

"Yes, in his capacity as our heir to High Meadows, William will announce to the servants what has happened, and that he will take over running the estate for the foreseeable future. He will apologize for the required haste of our departure, and assure all but one in our service that things will go on as usual."

"And that exception is Snead?"

"Precisely."

"But will William be able to drop his own business affairs so quickly?"

"Isabel, you would have been so proud of our son. We met in his office and Robert joined us. William said that he would do anything to aid us, and he envisions dividing his time between High Meadows and Winchester, for now. Eventually, he will make a choice of residence to suit his family. But he will manage both farm and business with any additional help that's needed."

"God bless him. All right, so Snead is to be dismissed?"

"Yes, and that is where William and Robert will assert authority. Snead will be instructed to accompany them to a private meeting in my study. He'll be told that William has decided to select his own overseer. Then Snead will be thanked for his service, and offered a generous severance payment of two month's wages and a good letter of reference."

"And if he still threatens to ruin us?"

"Robert will state that his claim is absurd, and that he is willing to put Snead in front of a judge for slandering us as a result of him being dismissed. Furthermore, he'll tell Snead that if he persists, his reference will be withdrawn."

"Will the reference mean that much to him?"

"As disagreeable as he can be, Snead is no fool. With no job to fall back upon, a good reference will be invaluable to him."

"But if Robert and William can force him off, why cannot we just wait a time, and return?"

"The reality, my dear, is that if a man like Snead could gain the ear of my political rivals, a writer for a penny press, or even the local pattyrollers, we'd be endangered by returning too soon. If Snead suspects a ruse in our going north, it might trigger his actions. We will be much safer after he is well-settled in his next post."

"Six months, a year?" asked the mistress with wavering hope.

"For a good while, at least," replied Mr. Cauley.

# Chapter 49

Despite her concern and wonderment at what this secret meeting could be about, Auntie Dee did her best to appear unworried and cordial as Mr. and Mrs. Cauley entered the kitchen. Those requested to be there were already assembled.

"Hello, Mastah an' Mistress."

"Hello, Auntie, and hello to all," the master quietly said as he and Mrs. Cauley shuffled to find a position in the kitchen where they could clearly be seen by everyone present.

"Yes, hello, everyone. Thank you for coming on time," the mistress whispered. "Mr. Cauley has some important and exciting news to share with you!"

"Indeed," seconded the master. "I believe you all know that it has been my privilege to serve our commonwealth for many years. Now, I am very gratified to be asked to serve our nation, in the capital at Washington City. I will be joining my brother Stephen, there, as a special consultant to the government. And there is an urgency for us to leave immediately. We will depart at midnight, tonight, to make the journey."

"Mastah," said Auntie Dee with grave concern, "is yuh sayin' dat y'all gwan be leavin' us fuh good?"

"No, Auntie, because we want each of you here to *accompany* us."

There was a wide range of responses to the master's statement. Auntie Dee was both surprised and troubled. Aidan looked right away to Liza for her reaction, and was encouraged that she was calm, even pleased. Jack jumped up and down, saying, "I like Washington!" and had to be shushed. Essex praised God, and Chloe looked thunderstruck.

Then the mistress instructed, "We want you to accompany us, now, so that we can set up a household there. And we must not alert any of the others working at High Meadows of our preparations and departure. We don't want to cause undue disturbance and worrying overnight. Our son, William, will be here early tomorrow morning to explain this change to the others, and to take over running the farm just as we did. So we are doing all we can to make this a smooth transition for everyone."

"Yes," Mr. Cauley continued, "and when we adjourn here, we ask that you go back to your quarters, wait until others around you are asleep, and then quietly pack your personal effects and clothing. If anyone does see you, tell them not to worry, and to go back to sleep. Then bring your things back here to the kitchen until we are all ready to leave together.

"Aidan," continued the master, "I am sure that you have as many questions as anyone, and I will consult with you in a moment about what you should carry along to be able to continue your trade in Washington. Space will be at a premium, however. And we must enlist you, and you, Essex, to quietly remove several heavy trunks from the manse.

"The Lord is blessing us tonight with a good, strong moon to light our way. Our lanterns and the carriage lights will help. I'll lead our party on my horse. The mistress will ride in the carriage with Auntie and Chloe. Essex, you can drive them. And Aidan, I'll ask that you drive the wagon with Liza and young Jack.

"Now, this is very important. We will be going to a new place, and dealing with many new things. We'll be living either in or near a great city. And some of you may be leaving our home regularly on various errands. At such times, you may be approached by people who would encourage you to run away, and abandon your service to us. Faced with those circumstances, I feel bound to ask each of you this question. If we take you with us, do you swear now, in front of the Almighty and all those present, that you will remain our loyal servants? Liza?"

"Yes, of course, master. I must attend my lady."

"Excellent, Liza. And you, Auntie?"

Through tears, Auntie Dee sobbed, "Mastah, please ast me de las'."

"All right, then. Aidan, will you faithfully journey with us?"

"I am indentured to thee, sir. And I trust thee. Jack and I will faithfully come."

"Quite so, young Jack?"

"Quite so, sir."

"Essex?"

"I feels like Mr. Aidan do, Mastah."

The mistress interjected, "And Chloe, you have been with us such a short time. But we want you as part of our household."

"I trusts you, mistress. I hope you think my work is right."

"You are learning well, Chloe," Mrs. Cauley assured her.

Then the master tenderly returned to Auntie Dee. "Auntie, can you give me your answer now?"

"Oh, Mastah, I hope yuh knows how much I cares fuh yuh, an' Ms. Isabel. I always will. An' dere ain't neber gwan be no question 'bout me bein' loyal. Yuh bot' de bes' t'ing ebuh happen ta Auntie Dee. But yuh doesn't need me up dere in Washington."

Mrs. Cauley moved quickly to Auntie Dee's side and hugged her. "Oh, of course we'll need you, Auntie," the mistress said. "We could never imagine not having you with us."

"Dat mean mo' ta me dan yuh ebuh know, Mistress. But where yuh be up dere in de capital gwan call fuh *fancy* cook, can make all kind o' French dis an' dat."

The master strongly asserted, "The fare you've prepared for our table has *never* cast shame on our household, Auntie Dee. Quite the opposite."

"I hopes so. T'ank yuh, Mastah. But my heart say stay here, too, on account o' de ones yuh be leavin' behind. I learnt dat dere's one t'ing 'bout slabes on a plantation. Dey always has ta hab somebody ta turn tuh when dey sick, when dey sad, an' when dey needs ta be set right. I knows, Mastah, yuh an' Ms. Isabel gwan do dat fuh all dem what's goin' wit' yuh."

"But Auntie," the mistress pleaded, "surely someone else can fill that role here."

"Can dey, Essex?" Auntie posed through a sniffle.

"Um, ain't none I knows of Auntie Dee."

Liza nervously interrupted, "Master and Mistress, may I speak with Auntie Dee outside for a moment?"

The master said, "Certainly, Liza. We can give you a few minutes. Just keep your voices low."

Liza ushered a curious Auntie Dee out of ear shot outside, and firmly, but quietly said, "Auntie, do you remember what you told me in that very kitchen when I had doubts about ever becoming a real lady?"

"Shuh, Miss Liza. But what dat hab ta do wit' Auntie Dee?"

"It has *everything* to do with you. You said it yourself, just now. You're afraid that your cookin' won't be *fancy* enough for important visitors up in Washington."

"Well it won't!"

"How do you know? And where's the faith in that?"

"What?"

"You told me don't ever let my doubts beat me down, because I owed it to all of us to live up to being the best I can."

"Da's right. So what?"

"So what about you? Don't you believe in what you're preachin'?"

"Oh Liza, stop makin' so much sense."

"Know what it's going to take for you to stay on here? No sense at all!

"Now get in there, Auntie, and tell master and mistress you want to go with them and serve them well. If you don't, you'll always regret it. And the master can't wait any more for you to wobble around thinkin' about it."

With that, Liza marched back into the kitchen, crossed her arms in front of her, and said, "Thank you Master and Mistress."

Soon she was followed by a repentant Auntie Dee who said, "Mistress and Mastah, I done thought some muh on dis chance yuh gibin' me ta start new life wit' y'all. Mastah

William a good, young Christian man. He take good care res' o' de slabes. So, dat's it. Auntie Dee comin' wit' yuh."

Mrs. Cauley kissed Auntie Dee's glistening face as everyone else had to stifle cheers of joy!

As the secret meeting wound down, Aidan and Essex took their instruction from the master, and Liza and Chloe escorted the mistress back to the manse.

Then Liza told Chloe what to pack for their fast-approaching journey.

# Chapter 50

Of all the beloved friends and grand people that Jack and Aidan met at High Meadows, perhaps no one touched their hearts more than young Chloe. Her life, though short in years when they met, showed the stark contrast between the worst evils of slavery, and what it is like to be treated with a measure of kindness by people like the Cauleys.

Make no mistake, Aidan never believed that it was right for any man or woman to be owned by another human being. Even under what he and Jack considered to be their favorable living conditions, Aidan still felt robbed of his full dignity, by owing ten years of his life in service to another man.

He felt that way despite the fact that he and Jack had a real advantage in keeping their spirits up compared to the true slaves. As indentured servants, they knew the term of their servitude was certain to end. That gave Aidan and Jack a powerful tool. It gave them hope.

Slaves only know that they *want* freedom. But how do you gain it, when you need a piece of paper to give you permission to walk a country path? How do you get it, when you can't even read what's on the note? How do you reach freedom, when trying to escape will risk your life? And would you take the risk knowing, that if caught, your punishment will be so severe, you'll wish you'd been shot in the back of the head on the run?

Still, there are degrees of degradation. And where Christ's light shines, the most evil darkness cannot prevail.

That light shone through a vivid account given by Chloe at her fireside, years after the night she was supposed to flee to Washington City in the Cauley's coach. And just like her first conversation with Auntie Dee in her kitchen, Chloe shared that story with a guest over a fresh cup of hot tea.

"Well, dat night, afta' meetin' wit' de mastah an' mistress in Auntie Dee's kitchen, Miss Liza tell me what ta put in a sack dat she give me up de big house. Soon as I lef' her an' was on de path, almos' ta my cabin, Snead de overseer jump out an' grab me!

"No!"

"Um hmm. He put his hand over my mouth and tell me *hush!* I could smell de whiskey on him.

"He say, 'Well, Chloe, my sweet thing, before sundown tomorrow, I'll know that you're gonna be my personal maid, all nice an' cozy-like. You will cook for me, clean for me, and you'll meet my needs at night.'

"Lord, no!" cried Chloe's companion.

"I was so scared," Chloe admitted, "couldn't say nothin'—jus' trembles.

"Then he say, 'Why don't you give me a little kiss to hold me over until tomorrow night?'

"Den he take me by de shoulders an' tries force a filthy kiss on me. I screams loud as I can, '*Brister!*'

"Sho' nuff, my brother come flyin' up de path an' launch hisself at Snead! Snead lef' go o' me ta draw his pistol, but Brister knock him down. Snead quicker'n I thought, though, an' he jump up an' pull his gun, while Brister flash a big knife and stab it in Snead belly!"

"Did that kill him?"

"Jus' wait!" Chloe said. "Same time Brister stab him, Snead shoot an' hit Brister in de leg! But Brister stab him two mo' time fo' Snead hit de ground. I jus' stan' screamin' while Brister fall down from de gunshot.

"He layin' dere hold his leg an' say ta me, 'See if he dead!'

"Was he?"

"Wait," Chloe said again. "By dat time, slave name Essex come a-runnin'. 'You all right, boy?' Essex say.

"'Jus' shot in de leg, but bleedin' bad,' Brister say.

"'Come on den,' Essex say, while he pick up Brister in his arms. 'I gits ya back ta Auntie Dee.'

"Essex seen de knife in Snead, so he kick him. Snead mouth drop open.

"Essex say, 'He dead.'

"Finally!"

"All right!" Chloe agreed. "So now we takin' Brister back up de kitchen an' meet Mr. Aidan an' Jack on de way. Jack jus' a little boy back den. We sees mo' slave come a-runnin' an' mastah an' mistress comin' ta meet Auntie Dee outside de kitchen.

"Mastah see Brister an' say, 'What happened to him?'

"I say, 'Snead shot him in de leg, Mastah. Snead try ta force hisself on me an' I calls fo' Brister. He pulls gun on Brister an' shoots, but Brister stab him dead.'

"Den all de women screams! But Auntie Dee say, 'Fo'gib me Jesus, but *praise God Almighty*!'

"Ha, ha!"

Chloe laughed, too, then said, "So, Mr. Aidan say, 'Bring Brister in the kitchen!'

"He clears off Auntie Dee's kneadin' table so's Essex can lay Brister on it. Den Mr. Aidan cuts off Brister pants leg. He tie two kerchief together, rolls 'em like a rope, an' tie it 'round Brister leg ta stop de bleedin'. It work. He save Brister life."

"Thank God."

"Really thank God cause, up ta den, Brister don't want nothin' ta do wi' Mr. Aidan cause he white."

"Um."

"Anyways, Auntie clean up de blood, an' somebody say, 'Good. De bullet gone clean through de muscle an' don't hit no bone.'

"Jus' ta make sho', mastah ast Brister real slow move his leg dis way an' dat. He done it, an' everbody happy.

"So Auntie give him little glass whiskey drink. She wait awhile. Den she pat some whiskey on where de bullet go in, and where it come out. He bite his lip so's he don't scream. Den she wrap de leg wi' bandage.

"Afta all dat, mastah give us a speech. By now, everbody else on de whole place standin' outside lookin' in de windahs, lookin' in de do'.

"So mastah say loud enough could everbody hear, 'I need for everyone to understand, and always remember exactly what happened here tonight. Phineas Snead was trying to take liberties with young Chloe. Chloe, did you lead that man on in any way?'

"I say, 'No, Mastah. He jump out de bushes an' try'n force hisself on me. Den I screams fo' Brister.'

"Mastah say, 'Chloe, repeat what you told us here before.'

"So I did.

"Den mastah say, 'This, then, was a clear case of Brister's self-defense. If anyone here is asked what happened tonight, remember what Chloe has said. Snead assaulted her, Brister came to her aid, Snead drew on Brister to kill him, and Brister did what he had to do to save himself.'

"Den all de slaves says, 'Amen' and some other things 'bout how Snead have it comin'.

"Next thing is when mastah say, 'And, I have other important news to share. Mrs. Cauley and I have been considering whether to accept an invitation to move to the capital, at Washington City, to do important government work there.'

"When he say dat, all de slave starts moanin' till mastah raise his hand. Den he say, 'But the Lord has shown us, quite clearly, that we are meant to stay right here with you at High Meadows.'

"Shoot, you'd o' thunk it was de Fourth o' *Ju*-ly! Since half us was already in de kitchen where Auntie keep de wine an' spirits locked up, mastah say, 'Why don't we have a little toast to Mrs. Cauley's and my homecoming?'—even though dey ain't even lef' for nowheres! Den dat little toast lead to another, an' another.

"Some time afta' dat, somebody remembers we still has a dead body ta bury. By den, mastah's spirits runnin' high, an' he say somethin' like, 'With as much respect for the departed as I can muster, and in consideration of the fact that, to the best of my knowledge, there is no immediate next of kin to notify, I believe that we can proceed with the interment immediately.'

"So somebody ast, 'Mastah, wha's dat mean?'

"So mastah say, 'That means two or three able-bodied men can grab a shovel. We're going to plant Mr. Snead *tonight*!'

"Everbody start ta cheer and volunteer dig de hole! Dat were de mos' happiest night o' my life, up to now. An' it were de happiest night o' mos' everbody at High Meadows. One mo' thing. It de firs' time I eva' seen Miss Liza kiss Mr. Aidan. An' it were a good one, too!"

"That's beautiful!"

"Yes, well, dat musta' inspire Mr. Aidan, cause he got us all ta singin' 'round a big bonfire all dem song he help us wrote. We sung 'em almos' all night long. An' de mastah an' mistress was dere fo' mos' of it. An' it were de firs' time I eva' sung de song *I* wrote. Was scared ta sing it, but I done it. Den we all cried. But afta', we all feel good. It tell how I missed my baby girl."

Then Chloe asked tentatively, "You want ta hear it?"

"Yes. I'd like that very much!"

"Okay," Chloe solemnly replied, as she took a deep breath. "Go like dis."

Hid From Sight (Slow Tempo)

Sittin' at de river's edge
A little life on my mind,
Bore dat chile but now I know
She never gwan ta be mine.

Each time de father come ta me
Pray dat he don't return,
But baby born wi' skin so white
Big house all startin' ta burn!

CHORUS

Oh will I eva' see de chile
Made on dat horrible night?
Will I have ta wait until
We ge's ta de nex' life?
Some peoples say don't worry
Li'l gal gwan be all right,
Lawd, wrap an' keep you arms around
De chile dey hid from sight.

Mastah keep a mammy nurse
Some place way far from here,
She come one day by wagon
An' I say, "I wants ta see her."

Put my baby to her breas'
Chile don't know hers from mine,
But when dat wagon lef from here
I heard my baby cryin'!

*CHORUS*

*Oh will I eva' see de chile*
*Made on dat horrible night?*
*Will I have ta wait until*
*We ge's ta de nex' life?*
*Some peoples say don't worry*
*Li'l gal gwan be all right.*
*Lawd, wrap and keep you arms around*
*De chile dey hid from sight.*
*Oh wrap and keep you arms around*
*My baby, dey took cause she look white.*

As Chloe finished singing, she and her guest tightly embraced and rocked back and forth as they sobbed uncontrollably.

After several minutes, the beautiful young woman finally caught her breath enough to cradle Chloe's face in her hands and whisper, "Oh Momma, I love you, and how I missed you so!"

CPSIA information can be obtained
at www.ICGtesting.com
Printed in the USA
LVOW04s1530190116
471354LV00018B/941/P

9 780615 992532